Mum's Army

Love and Adventure From the NAAFI to Civvy Street

Winifred Phillips

with

Shannon Kyle

SIMON &
SCHUSTER

London · New York · Sydney · Toronto · New Delhi

A CBS COMPANY

First published in Great Britain by Simon & Schuster UK Ltd, 2013
A CBS COMPANY

1 3 5 7 9 10 8 6 4 2

Simon & Schuster UK Ltd
1st Floor
222 Gray's Inn Road
London WC1X 8HB

www.simonandschuster.co.uk

Simon & Schuster Australia
Sydney

Simon & Schuster India
New Delhi

A CIP catalogue record for this book is available from the British Library.

ISBN 978-1-47111-125-9

Typeset in Bembo by Hewer Text UK Ltd, Edinburgh
Printed in the UK by CPI Group UK Ltd, Croydon CR0 4YY

While this book gives a faithful account of the author's experiences, some
names have been changed to protect the privacy of the individuals involved.

Contents

Contents

Prologue

'Upstairs to your bedroom. NOW!'

My mother's eyes were flashing as she pointed her index finger towards the ceiling.

I glared at her with all the indignation a five-year-old could muster.

'It wasn't me, it was Cliff!' I screamed back, running upstairs as fast as I could. I slammed my bedroom door, my heart beating so loudly it sent a whooshing to my ears. Shaking with rage, I glanced at the bedroom window.

She's not going to lock me in here, I thought defiantly, running over to it.

With all my might, I shoved up the heavy sash window and, without thinking, sat on the sill, dangling my legs over the edge.

I could see our small grassy front garden around fifteen feet below. Again without a moment's thought, I shuffled my bottom further onto the edge of the sill, and suddenly I was in free fall, cool air whipping my hair up skyward.

For a split second I felt as free as a bird. But as I fell, something ripped loudly.

Landing in a heap on the lawn, I stared down at the fabric of my dress now in two halves, flapping open in the breeze. It had caught on the window opening but in my joy of escaping I'd not even noticed.

Mum would be even crosser with me now. But it didn't stop me from smiling.

Nothing can stop me, I thought, triumphantly. I did it! I looked back up at the wide-open window, so pleased with myself.

I could hear Mum clattering about in the kitchen, getting dinner on. She'd always been a good cook, if nothing else. Delicious smells of bread, casseroles or cakes were always emanating from the cooker. Mum was famed in our neighbourhood in Ilford, east London, for being able to make something out of nothing. Which was just as well, as my dad was never around. He worked in Coventry, as a Post Office engineer and we rarely saw him. He just popped in and out, setting the pattern for the rest of our lives.

I liked sitting on this lawn, hugging my knees, contemplating how I'd managed to give Mum the slip. It was my brother Cliff's fault anyway. Younger than me by twenty months, Cliff could wind me up rotten, and I didn't deserve such a telling-off.

Well, I wasn't going to be banished to my bedroom, not for him, not for anyone.

Then our neighbour's face popped over the fence.

'You all right, Win?' she asked, her brows knotted. 'What you doing down there?'

'I jumped,' I beamed, pointing at the window.

'You what?' she said, turning pale, her face tightening with concern. We both looked up at my bedroom curtain now swaying in the breeze out the window.

'From all the way up there?' she gasped.

'Yes!' I giggled. 'And it didn't even hurt.'

In an instant, the neighbour was hammering at our door and I could hear Mum's voice shrieking.

'WINI-FRED!' she screamed. 'GET YOURSELF BACK INDOORS NOW. WHAT THE HELL ARE YOU PLAYING AT?'

And I was dragged back inside for a dressing-down. But as Mum ranted and raved, I just stared at her wondering where I could next escape. Where and when . . .

Chapter One

Bumpy Journey

Right from the start life wasn't all happy families for me. My mother, Doris Guest, married my father, Sydney James Phillips, in Barford register office, Nottingham & Derby County, when she was seventeen and he was twenty-two.

I never knew my maternal grandparents, but they are named on the marriage certificate as Mary Elizabeth Guest (nee Duggins) and Harry Guest, an ironworker.

From the beginning I don't think my parents' marriage was a match made in heaven. Mum was a beautiful lady with dark hair and pretty eyes but she never seemed happy. Dad was a balding man with glasses and a wide-open face and he seemed to come and go whenever he pleased. I was their baby number three after my two other brothers, Norman and Ken. After me came Cliff.

Norman was ten years older than me and went to work as a milkman after leaving school at fourteen. Ken, seven years older than me, was still at school. We knew my paternal grandparents, but didn't have much to do with them. Grandma (Minnie) Phillips was a force to be reckoned with. She hated my mum, and wasn't afraid to show it. I remember her screaming at Mum to get me checked by a doctor after my adventure falling out of the window, but I didn't much like her. A dour woman, she didn't seem to have much time for us kids.

Soon after this incident, when I was still about five, we moved into a downstairs flat in Ilford, near a railway line. My younger brother Cliff, then a toddler, was playing on the path outside our front door, running up and down the path.

'Neeee naaaaw, neeeee naaaaaaw,' he cried, as he went backwards and forwards. I didn't take much notice until I heard the most ear-shattering crash. Then a sickening pause, before a huge wail.

Poor Cliff had smashed head-first into the glass front door, going straight through. His hands were covered in shards of glass, cut to ribbons.

'Muuum!' I screamed. My poor brother was oozing with bright-red blood. Mum came running out and an ambulance was called. It wasn't to be the last scrape Cliff would be in either. He was so accident prone and a worry to us all. He had scars on his hands from that accident right up until the day he died.

Around this time, Norman also fell ill and had to have time off work, staying in bed with a sweaty brow, moaning with fever.

'What's wrong with him, Mum?' I'd ask, listening to him breathing heavily.

'It's that water tank,' Mum kept muttering. 'That's what's made him sick.'

Thankfully, Norman recovered and went back to work, which as far as Mum was concerned was a good job, as she needed the money.

She never said much, but she'd often have to make food stretch and one chicken could be turned into many dinners. Dad came and went and although nobody said anything, it must've been an unusual household for an area where everyone else seemed to have a dad who not only lived with them but worked all day too.

One morning, Mum packed small cases for us.

'You're going on a train,' she said simply, as she hurriedly emptied our drawers. She was folding all our clothes very fast and really squashing them down. 'Ken is going to look after you for the journey.'

Even though I'd no idea what was going on, I felt a cold hard knot form in the pit of my tummy. I knew better than to ask questions though. You didn't ask questions in those days. You just did what you were told, when you were told.

The look on Ken's face told me it was bad news, but again, I felt too scared to ask.

Cliff and I had our coats put on and we were bundled up the front path. Mum waved goodbye briskly and our front door clicked shut.

Ken walked us to the train station; he was only about thirteen himself. Tears were shining in his eyes.

'Hold my hand,' he said to Cliff, who started crying as he walked.

Our little footsteps were swiftly made in silence, and then I realised tears had started to pour down my cheeks too. Ken stiffly asked the ticket man at the station for three seats to Coventry, handing over the money and trying to look grown-up.

'Are we going to see Daddy?' I finally spluttered. All I knew of Coventry was that he lived there sometimes.

Ken nodded, sniffing and wiping his nose on his sleeve. 'We're leaving home,' he cried. 'And I don't think we'll be going back!'

My eyes rounded with horror, but before I had a chance to ask anything else, the train had arrived and doors were opening. We climbed on board, along with commuters and other families. Mums and dads seemed to be everywhere, gently holding their children by the hand or sitting them on their knees. Noses were being wiped, biscuits handed out. Everyone looked quite normal, just busy or content, going somewhere for the day or heading home.

But we were all crying. We'd no idea where we were going or what was to become of us.

Ken tried to control Cliff's screams as the train pulled away.

I sat and hid my face in my hands as big sobs heaved at my chest. Somehow I knew there and then Mum didn't want us. Somehow I knew we'd been abandoned. I was being sent away. It's a feeling that's stayed with me for the rest of my life.

I stared out of the window smeared with soot, watching as familiar streets and houses slipped by and then disappeared completely. They were soon replaced with unfamiliar rolling green fields and a grey sky to match all our moods.

Wherever we were going and whatever was going to happen I couldn't change, so I just tried not to think about it.

After a few hours and a couple of changes we pulled into Coventry and piled off the train. I took Cliff's hand as Ken struggled with our bags, all knocking against his skinny legs.

We stumbled along the platform, hearts in our mouths, wondering what was going to happen next. And then a man emerged from the crowds with a familiar bald head and glasses. I knew this man was my dad, but I didn't really 'know' him.

'You're coming with me,' he smiled, as he took our bags. 'Did you have a good journey?'

Once again, nothing was explained.

I can't remember much of this stay, we must have gone to Dad's house, but I've no recollection of any of it. Very shortly afterwards, I was told I was going to Auntie Annie's house in Canterbury. I'd heard of this auntie before, but up until then had no proper memories of her. She was almost a stranger really.

'She'll take good care of you, Win,' beamed Dad, as if it was the most exciting thing in the world to happen to me.

Only afterwards did I discover where my brothers ended up. We didn't see much of each other for years afterwards. Ken stayed with my dad in Coventry, Cliff went to Mansfield where he stayed with Grandma Phillips, and Norman left home. We were scattered to the winds, family life never to be the same again and we just had to accept it.

Auntie Annie was married to my father's brother Percy. Originally Annie Dickens, she'd lived in Canterbury all her life, her father was an alderman on the council, and she had three children: Maisie, seventeen, Nora, nineteen (who was away working as a nanny) and fourteen-year-old George.

When I arrived at Annie's, at St Martin's Road, Canterbury, I didn't know what to expect. I was so happy to find it was a warm and loving home. Annie was a tall, plump lady who always wore smart knee-length flowery tea dresses, and seemed very happy to have me there.

'You're going to find a home here all right, Winifred,' she said to me kindly. In comparison to my mother, who was always a little bit distant, this lady seemed like an angel.

There was a big area at the back of the house and Annie's family owned the land behind all the way up to No. 37. It was a bit of grass with lots of trees and, being the tomboy I was, I soon discovered I loved climbing them.

Auntie Annie ran a sweet shop on Broad Street in Canterbury, which was every child's idea of heaven. Filled with tall jars standing neatly on shelves, right up to the ceiling, it was a colourful place and smelled deliciously of burned sugar at all times. Sometimes, for fun, Annie asked me to go under the counter and look for any coins that had rolled under there.

I'd come out with dusty knees, beaming, holding a few pennies. Then she'd let me choose any sweets I liked, usually boiled sweets or toffees. Strangely, I didn't like chocolate back then!

Annie was a very generous lady, well liked in the area. Her warm nature meant she could never see anyone go without. If anyone who was ill walked into the shop she'd not hesitate to pull up a small table and chair, and then ladle some soup into a bowl. She always had something going on the stove in the back of the shop, just in case.

'There you go,' she'd smile. 'This will make you feel better.'

And there were plenty of people in the 1930s who were grateful for her help. Many were wandering around ill at that time. There was a recession, high unemployment and little welfare provision. By 1931, the result of the 1929 stock market crash in America had spread to the rest of the world and by the end of this year a fifth of the workforce in the UK was unemployed. Soup kitchens sprang up in many cities just to stop people starving on the streets. Often it was the kindness of local people who helped those in need of something to eat or a kind word or two.

Sometimes Auntie Annie would put me on the high wooden counter in the shop and ask me to dance. I was a little diva really and loved prancing and dancing around to old music-hall songs at the time. I loved making people laugh, feeling like the centre of attention. I suppose it was because I'd rarely got much attention up to this point.

I might have looked like a happy child to the outside world back then. But inside, I don't think anything could've made me feel happy or like I truly belonged. I missed my brothers, but no one ever explained anything about what had happened and I knew better than to ask. I missed my mum, even though she'd not been much of a mother to me;

she was who I belonged to. But now it was clearly evident that wasn't the case. I didn't know if I'd ever see her again and nobody spoke about her.

Shortly after arriving I was taken to an elementary school for my first day by Maisie. She walked me there and then dropped me off at the gate.

'See you later,' she smiled, waving at me.

She must've thought it was obvious I was being picked up later, but to my young mind it wasn't. I thought she was dumping me somewhere strange again and I feared being deserted.

Oh no! I thought, as she turned her back. This is happening all over again! I'm being left behind!

Again, I didn't cry out or say anything. And I was very relieved to see her at the school gate afterwards, and clutched her hand tightly as we walked home.

My memories of this school are very hazy, but I wasn't there for long. Just a few months later, Auntie Annie patiently explained I would be going to a convent school nearby, the same one her daughters had been to years earlier.

'This is the right thing to do, Win,' she said, patting my hand.

And, like everything else, I just had to accept this.

I was to be a full-time boarder, so there from Christmas to Easter and not returning during term time at all. Of course, I'd prefer to have gone back to Auntie Annie's, but I didn't ask. Already, I was used to events being out of my control.

At the time, I thought I hated the convent, but looking

back we made our own fun. It was a cold, austere-looking building in beautiful grounds filled with cherry trees. The girls' dormitory was the part built to look like a castle. The nuns had another building attached, and were always nearby to keep a close eye on us.

My best friend there was a girl called Joan Grant. A pretty brunette, she was always up for a giggle. She was also a full-time boarder, so was around all weekends like me. I didn't know her family background and we never ever spoke about why we were there. In those days you didn't talk about personal things, even with friends. We just knew we had no mum or dad to look after us like the others and that was that.

I didn't care that much for working at school, although I enjoyed writing and soon found myself to be very clever at spelling in particular! I also discovered I loved geography, especially reading about other cultures and looking at maps; the world was such an enormous place. I often found myself staring at a world map on the wall, day-dreaming about places oceans away from Canterbury and Coventry.

One day . . . one day, I thought. I'd like to see some of it.

Strangely, I had a phobia about the paper I was writing on touching my hand. So I worked out how to write resting my hand on a wooden ruler. The teachers didn't approve of this and would bellow across the room if they caught me.

'Winifred!'

I'd jump out of my skin, as they'd whip the paper from under me.

'I don't want to do it now,' I'd argue, folding my arms across me. Right from then, I learned to know my own mind and if I didn't want to do something I could be rather difficult.

Although I didn't see my auntie until the holidays, I never felt rejected by her. She'd welcome me back with a warm hug and make me lovely dinners, always making sure I was fit to bursting.

Often, during term time, I'd spot her driving up the hill near the convent when she visited her daughter Nora, who by now had got married to Harry.

I'd be going for a walk with my class along the pavements in a strict crocodile line, when Auntie would drive past in her Austin 7, giving me a 'toot-toot' on her horn.

I'd look up and give her a wave back when the nuns weren't looking, feeling happy she was thinking of me.

Auntie Annie was a very protective mother, and she bought properties for all her children to live in once they were older, and would go and visit them regularly.

I was often taken on holidays during the summer months with the family. Uncle Percy would pile up the Austin with small bags and we'd set off to places like Brighton or Torquay for little breaks by the sea. This was quite far to go in those days! I think this added to my thirst for adventure and to see the world. I noticed how accents changed the further away we drove, how the colour of the bricks of houses were different, how the air smelled differently by the sea. These experiences made me long for more.

As for my parents, Dad only visited me a few times. I'd since learned they'd separated and that's why Mum had sent us kids off to live with relations. Mum visited me only once. One day, out of the blue, Auntie Annie just said: 'Incidentally, your mum is coming this afternoon for a little visit, Win.' It didn't upset me as by then I'd detached myself from her so much. By now she was just a woman, not my mum.

She came to visit all smartly dressed and smiling.

We stood awkwardly at the door for a moment before she firmly clasped my hand and took me out shopping for the day in Canterbury. I don't remember much, just walking round the shops with her as we made small talk. As we gazed in one shop window, full of lovely things, I looked longingly at a bag. It was one of those that looked like it had been knitted with silver. Very fashionable at the time.

'I'd love one of those,' I sighed.

And without hesitation she jumped in and bought it for me. It was only the second thing I'd ever been given by her. On another occasion, when I was very little, she'd handed me a small gold watch. I kept that by my bed and never wore it; it was more of a keepsake.

After her visit, I wasn't especially upset about her going. I'd grown to expect it now. Auntie Annie just made an extra fuss of me over dinner and made sure I was tucked up for bed afterwards.

The visits from Dad were slightly more frequent at school but always short and awkward – with stilted, polite conversations and stiff handshakes at the end. I felt detached from both parents now. After all, what kind of mum and dad were they to me? We'd become nothing but strangers by then.

On the odd occasion, I got to visit Cliff at my grandparents in Mansfield. And sometimes I had to go and stay with Dad in Coventry. By now he'd hooked up with a new lady friend, a widower called Olive. She was a round-faced fat lady who was always very stern with me. She had a look in her eye that told me she'd kill me if she could've got away with it! All she seemed to say was 'Winifred, do this' or 'Don't do that'. She showed no interest in me otherwise. She had a daughter though, called Margery, who was a few years older than me but absolutely lovely, a complete contrast to her mum. She always had time to chat and take an interest in me.

Although visits to see Dad were few and far between, there was one particular visit I've never forgotten. I was packed into the car with Dad and we drove off with him looking particularly grim.

'Where are we going, Dad?' I asked.

'You'll see when we get there,' he said. 'A solicitor's office.'

I didn't know what that meant, but I also knew from his tone that it was better not to ask.

Arriving at an austere-looking building in Birmingham, we got out and walked into an office off a place called 'The Judge's Chambers'.

Dad knocked on the door and ushered me into a room. A serious-looking older man was sitting behind a desk. I had to sit in a hard fancy wooden chair next to Dad, my feet almost dangling off the floor.

The man, a solicitor, shook Dad's hand and then carried on writing on some papers.

As we waited for him to finish, Dad fidgeted in his seat.

'Right,' said the man, finally, clearing his throat. He peered at me over his glasses. Then he clasped his hands in front of him, making a steeple out of his fingers.

'Winifred,' he said, 'we're here to decide who you want to live with. Your mother . . .' Then he glanced at Dad. 'Or your father?'

My heart started speeding up straight away, boom, boom, boom.

'You have to decide who would provide the best upbringing for you. You have to make a choice about what each parent could provide. Your father can provide a good, solid, stable home . . .' His voice just tailed off as my father sat watching me very carefully.

My heart was banging in my head so loudly now, I could barely hear anything at all. I covered my ears and squeezed my eyes shut.

'Stop, STOP!' a voice shouted. Then I realised it was my own.

I glanced at the door, resisting the urge to run out. Then I peered at the solicitor's big oak desk, covered in papers, files, a posh lamp. I knew if I had anything in my hand I'd have thrown it hard at him.

'Leave me alone!' I shouted, my voice now strong and clear. 'Let me live as I am!'

Dad sucked his lips in, and the solicitor looked taken aback. The pair of them ushered me out of the room as they carried on speaking. I didn't know what to think. What a question to have asked me! At the end of the day neither Mum nor Dad were real parents to me. I felt horrible inside. It was a choice but with no real choice.

The case was closed there and then. I was to live with my dad, although he never talked to me again about it.

In any case, I was back at school in Canterbury that Monday morning, just as if nothing had happened.

Chapter Two

Growing Pains

Although the nuns were not in any way violent, we were very clear about who was in charge of us at the convent. On the whole they were quite friendly, the Notre Dame Dominican order, but you were expected to do what you were told, no questions asked. Of course, we got away with things behind their backs wherever possible.

There was a farm over the back of the convent, filled with apple trees. So when the time was right and the boughs were heavy with ripe fruit, we'd flit over the fence at a quiet moment and help each other to climb the trees, pulling at the stalks and filling our skirts with fruit.

Then we'd collapse on the grassy banks and eat with the juice dribbling down our chins until we were full.

'This is the life!' said Joan with a wink. We liked being outside in the fresh air, with the smells of the nearby farm. It meant freedom to us.

Joan and I were friends right from the start when I was about six until we left at thirteen. As we blossomed into little ladies, she loved getting us to pose in the big mirror in the living room when no one was looking. She'd pull up her skirt slightly so I could admire her legs.

'Look at us, Win,' she laughed, turning this way and that. 'Look how pretty we are!'

I just laughed at her. But we were growing up fast and I couldn't wait. I wanted to be a woman. I wanted to leave the convent. I felt like my life was on hold until this happened.

One thing I did enjoy was our end-of-term concerts. We'd stage a production in front of all the parents, or in my case Auntie Annie, dressing up and singing usually. It was a big occasion and the Reverend Mother would reward us with prizes of chocolate, although I still wasn't keen on it at the time. Every time I performed I always managed to spot Auntie Annie's face in the crowd. She was very good, never missing me in a single show.

During the shorter holidays like half term, when we didn't go home, the girls who stayed on would get together for a dance.

We'd pull a big gramophone outside down the steps towards the tennis court and hold each other as if we were boyfriend and girlfriend, then start spinning around to all the great 1930s tunes at the time, sung by stars like Al Bowlly or Bing Crosby. The nuns must have known but chose to turn a blind eye. Perhaps they felt sorry for us having to stay at school in the holiday.

At the convent I quickly discovered what sport I liked and didn't like. I loved netball and tennis, they were so much fun. But I absolutely loathed cricket. It seemed like such a boy's sport and not suitable for us girls. Even the word 'cricket' sounded like a masculine word to me!

Although I didn't see much of my brothers, I always wrote regularly to Ken and Norman. Norman had now signed up to the army and sometimes I went to visit Cliff in Mansfield. I still didn't like my Granny Phillips much. She was a hard woman and didn't have much time for me; there was no maternal instinct there. But I loved Cliff so much. We were really rather close at the time. After effectively losing our parents, we appreciated having each other. He was very much my little brother though, always rather impatient and immature.

During one visit, Cliff, who as I say was always rather accident prone, fell over in front of me and bumped his head on the pavement. He must have been only about seven or eight and ended up with a bit of an egg on his head. When I saw him hurt, I cried and cried. I couldn't bear to see my little brother in pain. It was almost like I felt it myself.

Poor Cliff was always in the wars. Once, Granny Phillips took him out in a spanking new suit to the local park and he ended up slipping on the bank by the duck pond and going right the way in.

By the time I was nine years old I really felt as if I knew my own mind and I decided I wanted to become a Roman Catholic. It was not only being in the convent that made me want to change, it was living with my Auntie Annie too, who was a Catholic herself.

I'd heard Annie had even been to Lourdes a few years

earlier. I wasn't sure why but it fascinated me how miracles could happen. On one of his visits, I told Dad of my plans.

He stared at me through his glasses at the end of his nose and started wagging his finger at me.

'Well, girl, if you become a Roman Catholic you will stay a Roman Catholic for the rest of your life,' he said.

I nodded. I've done just that.

As I approached my teens, life was to change yet again for me. And not for the better. Little did I know, but Auntie Annie had fallen ill. All I'd heard, during a visit to her house, was she wasn't there because she was in hospital.

I'd known something was wrong the last time I had visited a few months previously. Auntie had been quieter than usual and I was sure I caught her grimacing in pain a few times. But she carried on making her lovely dinners, asking me about school and my dad, as cheerful as anything. Like most things, illnesses were brushed under the carpet and not spoken about. Especially to children.

One afternoon, a lady from down the road called Kitty popped in. I didn't know why but I really didn't like her. There was 'something about her' that put me on edge. She always seemed to brighten when Uncle was in the room, especially when Auntie wasn't there too. I couldn't put my finger on it but I didn't like her attitude.

Auntie Annie was washing vegetables at the kitchen sink as Kitty stuck her head around the door.

'Cooee,' she said, grinning to Annie. 'How you doing?'

'Not too bad, not too bad,' said Annie, her hands full of

spuds. She let them drop into the sink as she turned to look at Kitty.

The pair of them chatted for a little while about other neighbours and how the shop was doing. Then Annie looked directly at Kitty. She looked more tired than usual, pale and thinner too. I wondered if she'd been sleeping properly.

'Look after him, won't you, Kitty? Look after him,' she murmured before turning back to the spuds.

Kitty's eyes were momentarily sad before they sparkled again. She ran her fingers through her hair.

'I promise I will, Annie,' she said. 'You have my word.'

I didn't know what she meant then. But sadly it wasn't to be long before I'd find out.

There was a lot of talk among the adults about the war. The Germans under Adolf Hitler were making aggressive demands on other countries and Neville Chamberlain had tried to find peace with Hitler after meeting him in Munich, but still the country was bracing itself for more news.

I'd heard so much about the horror of the last war. None of the details, I would just overhear adults in my family or friends' parents talk about how 'awful' the Great War was. I didn't know anyone who had died but it seemed like the huge loss of life had affected everyone, even if no one directly in my family. The thought of us going to war again excited me in a strange way, but at the same time it was a very frightening prospect. I'd hear talk about gas attacks and bombs. It all seemed like a world away from our quiet little street.

I could see how worried people were, but didn't really understand. I just knew people who'd lived through the Great War hadn't had much to eat and lots of lives had been lost.

In Christmas 1938, I went to stay with Maisie, who'd since married and moved out, during the holidays as Annie was still ill.

Maisie was very quiet that Christmas Eve. I thought she looked more pale than usual as she picked me up from school, but I just assumed it was the cold weather making her peaky. It was a stark, grey day and the light seemed to have gone from her eyes. But the preparations for the big day had still been made, presents were wrapped and all the usual plans in place. I couldn't wait. I loved Christmas, it was always a cheerful time of year in Annie's household. We were to have dinner at Auntie Annie's house, my Uncle Percy was going to help with the meal while she was poorly and we'd have decorations and presents like always. Dad always sent something down for me too.

I just assumed Maisie was upset about her mum being ill, as I was, so I went to bed early ready to rise in the morning to go to Mass on Christmas Day as usual. I took comfort in the traditions at this time and hoped by next year Annie would be right as rain again.

The following morning was another gloomy day but we all said 'Merry Christmas' to other neighbours and then walked to church to hear the sermons and sing hymns.

After the priest spoke about the nativity story and we'd sung a few hymns it was time to hear the announcements about people living in the parish. He started reading the list of people who were poorly or who'd died and needed our prayers.

I kicked my legs under the seat in front, thinking about what we were going to have for dinner as the priest's deep voice rang out. I loved a good roast with potatoes, and it wouldn't be long before Uncle Percy was carving it up.

Then, suddenly, the priest's words seemed to boom out loud as if he was shouting through a loudspeaker.

'And we remember Annie Phillips who sadly passed away last night in Kent and Canterbury hospital . . .'

I felt as if I'd been punched in the guts. I turned to look at Maisie – her lower lip was quivering but she didn't look in my direction. She just wiped her eye with her sleeve. Then she took my hand and squeezed it. I knew there and then she must've known Auntie Annie had died but couldn't find the words to tell me. Her heart was broken and she couldn't bear to break mine too.

So I said nothing. I sat back in the pew, hot tears pricking behind my eyes but never emerging.

Auntie Annie! I wanted to scream. Not my Auntie Annie!

By now I had been through enough. I'd started to disconnect with my emotions a little, so I just followed Maisie out of the church, copying the straight-backed fast pace she had.

We filed out with our brave faces firmly on, not catching any of our neighbours' sympathetic looks. Then we drove back in silence. As soon as I walked through Annie's front door though, I found tears slipping down my face despite myself. I just couldn't stop crying.

Uncle Percy ushered me in. The same old paper ring decorations hung across the living room, the same lights were on the tree. All the family was here, but the gap Annie had left was huge. I sat and looked at her empty chair and just sobbed. The others all cried too, I'm sure, but it was in private. Grief was a private thing then.

During dinner I was very quiet and couldn't help myself but cry as I watched Uncle carve the turkey and dish up the veg. How could poor Annie have gone so suddenly?

It should be Auntie, I thought over and over, as my plate was filled.

Despite trying to keep my brave face, more tears slipped down my nose. I just couldn't believe Annie was gone for ever. It seemed so cruel. Maisie and Nora tried to pat my hand, and pass me tissues.

'There, there, Win. Look what I've got for you!' Uncle said, brightly. He turned to the cupboard behind him and pulled out an envelope. I ripped it open to find a pound note from my dad.

'Happy Christmas,' his note read.

This was an enormous sum of money in those days. 'Thank you,' I whispered, my voice sounding hoarse.

The next day Uncle Percy told us we were going to see Auntie Annie in the morgue. We all sobbed quietly in the back seat of the car as we drove up there.

On arrival, a nurse ushered us in. I didn't know what to expect, but part of me desperately wanted to see my lovely auntie, just to try and understand what had happened.

Maisie held my hand as we followed the nurse down the corridor.

'She's not coming in,' said the nurse, pointing at me. 'Not a child.'

Maisie opened her mouth to argue but closed it again as she changed her mind.

'Yes I am!' I wailed. I was twelve years old, and I desperately wanted to go in.

'No, you're not,' said the nurse, gripping my hand. She opened the door for the others and they all trooped in to pay their final respects.

I started crying. I wanted Auntie Annie.

After Christmas we saw in the New Year of 1939, but it didn't feel like a time to celebrate. The talk of war was imminent. It wasn't a case of 'if' anymore but 'when' it broke out.

Within a year Uncle had married again. Kitty from next door became his wife. It was then their conversation as Auntie washed the vegetables sprang to my mind. She'd known, even back then, and had just wanted her much-loved husband cared for.

Chapter Three

At War

With the war on its way, and Auntie Annie gone, Dad decided he'd take me back to Coventry to start a new life with him. By now there wasn't anyone else to look after me, so I suppose he had no choice. It was sad saying goodbye, but I didn't have long to dwell on it. My life was about to change again and I had to focus on that!

By now Dad was officially living with Olive, even though they'd not wed yet. I couldn't have been less thrilled. She made no effort to get to know me, or care for me. She just told me off and glared at me whenever Dad left the room. I soon grew to deeply dislike her.

After being allowed to finish the school year at Canterbury, I was enrolled from September 1939 as a boarder at Our Lady's Convent boarding school in Southam, Rugby, a few miles away from where Dad was living.

It was very different from Canterbury, but I quickly made lots of friends, including a girl called Pat. She was a small, dark-haired pretty thing with a wicked sense of humour. There were quite a few younger kids there too, evacuees from some of the bigger cities.

Strangely enough, all of the nuns at the convent were German, but nobody made any comment about it. They were from the Sisters of the Poor Child Jesus. We were all victims of this war whatever our nationalities were.

One of the girls there was a very quiet blonde-haired Jewish German girl, who had been evacuated from her country. She slept at the other end of the dormitory from me, and always seemed to be a lone wolf, never saying boo to a goose. I often wondered how she felt about things and what her family were doing. It must've been so hard for her.

We were all given identity cards and gas masks in little cardboard boxes. Sometimes the nuns made us practise our gas-mask drill. They timed us as we put them on as fast as possible, and then made sure they fitted, with no gaps anywhere. The country was in great fear of a gas attack by the Germans and every child in the country had to carry one around their necks on pieces of string.

One thing we all loved doing was running into the tiny dairy they had there. It made all the butter and cream for the convent and sold some on to the local area. I loved running into the cool parlour, and when no one was looking we'd ask the maid if we could have a go on the heavy wooden handle used to stir the curds and whey. We'd stand and heave it around and around until our arms were tired as we stood on the cool stone floor. It was something different to do, something a little bit naughty, as we weren't supposed to be doing it.

* * *

I'll never forget the day 'war' broke out for us. I was in Coventry, staying with my father in the holidays before starting my new school. Life was fraught at home, and my relationship with Olive certainly hadn't thawed. I think by then, I'd grown so suspicious of my parents or anything to do with them, nobody could do enough for me. I was used to being second best.

Although I didn't see eye to eye with Olive, I'd grown quite close to Margery. She was just fantastic (and so unlike her mum!). We shared the same sense of humour, and even looked a bit alike. At seventeen, Margery was like my big sister. But she was so full of compassion for me, and always liked to help me out or tell me about her nights out dancing. I really looked up to her. Whereas her mother was always on at us kids, telling us not to do this or that, Margery was relaxed and happy. I felt a bit sorry for her too. She was often ill, and had to take to her bed sometimes.

Ken really liked her when he came to visit. In fact, the two of them grew rather close, always giggling together, heads down when people came into the room. Once Olive spotted, though, she went mad. 'Stop it, the pair of you!' she cried, pushing herself in between them. I don't think she liked the idea of them getting 'too close'.

That particular day Olive was cleaning the front windows on the terraced house they rented.

I was just hanging around outside, watching her. She was a rather fat lady and was huffing and puffing as she kept bending her back to dump the rag cloth into the bucket to soap up the water. I was sure she wanted me to help her, but that wasn't likely! I couldn't be bothered to try and score points with someone like her.

Then, all of a sudden, there came an almighty 'booming' sound. The windows literally rattled and the noise pounded my chest, and startled birds flew out of nearby trees. The noise came from the direction of the city and people started shouting as a plume of thick grey smoke billowed skywards.

Olive dropped the cloth she was holding and spun around, her face a puce colour. 'Oh my God!' she screamed. 'It's started! The war! Already!'

She dived inside, not even looking back to see what I was doing.

I looked on at her, and couldn't help almost laughing. To my child's mind, I wasn't scared in the least. I was excited! Something was happening at last and life was about to change. I suppose for me it could only change for the better, so it was something to look forward to rather than fear.

We ran indoors, and I watched in mild amusement as Olive ran around, slamming shut doors and windows, her eyes wild with terror.

'I can't believe the bombers are over here. They've reached here already. How did this happen?' she cried.

She turned on the wireless to hear any news, but it was just chat and records.

By the time Dad got home from work we discovered it wasn't the war at all. It was an IRA bomb, planted in the basket of a tradesman's bicycle. It had gone up in the town outside a shop called Astleys and had killed five passers-by, including a 21-year-old girl and a 15-year-old lad, and injured more than 100 people. There was a sense of relief mixed with horror that the IRA had started a mainland campaign as well.

'Terrible thing to have happened but at least it's not the real war yet,' said Olive to Dad that evening over dinner. 'But it's only a matter of time before that starts too.'

We carried on eating our shepherd's pie as the table fell silent. I wondered what it meant. War, when it was finally declared a week later, meant a whole new world.

For Christmas 1939 we spent the first family Christmas together. It was an exciting time for me, as I'd never remembered a family Christmas with my dad and Ken. By now Norman was away in the army, and had been posted to Palestine before the war. Cliff stayed in Mansfield, but just to have Ken and Margery joining us, I felt really happy.

We went for a walk after dinner together, linking arms like sisters, giggling away. Margery wanted to look after me, make sure I was OK and having fun, despite her mother's treatment of me. As we walked, chatting about boys and the weather and what presents we'd got, we bumped into a couple of soldiers on leave.

They gave us both a wink and stopped to talk. We felt so sorry for them; we wondered how well they were being treated, so we handed them over chocolates we'd got for Christmas, despite the rationing. They happily accepted them, but afterwards I wondered why we'd done that, when I discovered they probably had better rations than we did!

After Christmas, it was time, all too soon, to say goodbye. I felt a stab of envy that I couldn't stay at home like Margery did, but at the same time I longed to be away from Olive.

By now the war was in full swing. And Coventry was definitely on the German hit list! It was a good target as it was full of factories making munitions and components for transport like cars, aeroplanes and even bicycles, not to mention it had training bases for RAF aircraft.

The air raids began in earnest in 1940. Every night in the convent we could hear the sirens wailing and were ordered to dive under our beds as we listened to the distant booming of the bombs. During the heavier raids we had to run downstairs and lie down in the corridors. I don't recall a time when anybody cried or screamed. Even the little kids were calm and saw it as a bit of a game. I don't think they understood what was happening.

Although I appeared calm, inside I quaked and shivered like jelly as the booming sounds grew louder and more relentless. It was an unspoken fear: everyone was frightened, but we just sat it out together, telling each other stories, or just trying to go to sleep again if we were lucky.

The convent was on a hill, across the road from an airfield where the RAF practised their manoeuvres in their planes. This was a big target for the Germans and they were always trying to bomb it, sometimes dive-bombing and coming down very low.

I'd stick my fingers in my ears as I tried to block out the screaming of the planes' engines, followed by the inevitable whooshing and sickening explosions. Knowing it was probably ending someone's life was a horrible feeling. None of us even tried to look out of the windows to see anything. We were all too scared and the nuns told us never to look.

I knew my father was an ARP (Air Raid Precaution) warden and when he came to visit me some weekends, he told me how he was very busy at nights. I had stopped going to see him, but he carried on seeing me. I didn't dislike the man, but I just knew I didn't love him as a father. He'd take me out to tea sometimes, as that's all there was available now. With rationing, food was scarce, so a cup of strong tea and maybe a biscuit was all we could get. I suppose Dad did care for me in some ways. Once there were no buses to the convent and he could only get as far as Leamington, and had to walk from there. That was quite a distance, so he must have been determined to see me that day! I suppose he realised how badly Coventry might be affected by this war, and all too soon he'd be proved right.

On 14 November 1940, there was a huge air raid on Coventry, where so much was badly blitzed. I was lying in bed with a cold at the convent on the night. I had a mild fever, the shivers and a blocked nose, and felt very sorry for myself. The German girl also had a cold like mine and she was in bed too. Even though we were alone in our dormitory we still never spoke. She always looked so quiet, sad and distant. I wondered what was going on in her mind still.

That evening, as the sirens wailed, the nuns came rushing in.

'You two girls, you have to get out of bed now,' said one breathlessly. 'I know you're unwell but it's not safe in here.'

We grabbed our dressing gowns and with my head hammering with headache from the cold and tension from the air raid, we shuffled downstairs.

'It's going to be a busy night,' said one nun softly, patting my arm.

Already the business of air raids had become a fact of life I was quite used to!

But that evening it sounded like hell on earth outside. So many bombs, then silence, then more bombs. Coventry was about fourteen miles away, but we could tell it was being blasted to smithereens. I thought of Margery and my dad. I hoped they'd made it to a shelter. I pushed the thought from my mind.

'Of course they will have, Win,' I told myself firmly.

We listened as hour after hour it went on. It was just relentless. I wondered if the guns in the city had shot down any planes at all.

Afterwards all phone lines were down and it was hard to communicate with the outside world as people spent all their time clearing up the mess. I didn't know for a whole week whether my father was alive or dead.

I just waited patiently. News did filter through of the devastation the raid had caused. Over 500 German bombers had carried out the attack, and they'd targeted the water, electricity and gas supplies first and then followed this up with a devastating second-wave attack. More than 4,000 homes had been destroyed and even the cathedral set on fire! I also heard Coventry only had a few gunners on the ground and only one German plane was shot down. Basically, the city had been left defenceless and paid a heavy price. More than 500 people had perished.

'I wonder what's happened to my dad,' I said to some of the girls over lunch. I asked one of the nuns if there was any way of finding out.

'I am afraid, dear, nobody can find out anything,' she said. 'We just have to pray and wait.'

Already I'd learned as a child there was little point in fretting about things. For the whole of the next week I just kept telling people: 'I don't know about Dad yet.' That was all I could bring myself to say. What would be would be, I kept thinking, trying to blank out the worst. A week later I did hear he was safe and well. I was so relieved. The next time I saw him, he looked tired, but he never spoke about what had happened and I didn't ask.

Although Dad had escaped this time, there was more bad news. Margery had fallen ill again. I never knew exactly what; again, illnesses were not discussed in details, it was a private matter. But she was always chesty and I think it was TB, and she'd take to her bed for a few days.

When I was allowed, I'd pop in and see her to chat. She always had a kind word, even when she was suffering and her breathing wasn't good. But this time Dad said she wasn't right at all and the doctor had been called in the night.

'Let her know I'm thinking of her,' I said.

* * *

Life carried on at the convent and I simply couldn't wait until I was sixteen so I could try and escape. I didn't know what to do but I knew I didn't want to stay a moment longer with the nuns!

Then one day one of the older girls, Maisie Reeve, came to visit us. She often popped into the church, saying hello to everyone. Maisie had left the convent a few months earlier to go into nursery-nurse training. It meant going on a two-year course, to learn how to look after babies and younger children.

'Do you like it, Maisie?' I asked. I was intrigued. Most of us girls stayed at the convent until eighteen and then did whatever our parents decided. Often girls just got married, but now the war was on, many were told to go and work in munitions factories or join in the war effort on the land. For many people our age there was very little choice as to which path you took in life.

To me, Maisie appeared like a pioneer, someone who was making her own journey in life, and I admired this so much. She seemed to enjoy nursing and revelled in the independence. This appealed to me very much.

In a quiet moment, I couldn't help quizzing her about her new life.

'It's hard work,' she smiled. 'But fun at times too. I'm just so happy to know I'll be earning my own money. And putting something towards the war effort.'

I asked her a few more questions, like how to get on the course, who could apply and whether I stood a chance.

'I don't see why not, Win!' she said. 'You'd be perfect, I'm sure.' She went on to tell me how to apply.

I felt so excited, I could barely contain myself, as the nuns hushed at us to be quiet. Now I had a plan, I was going to apply to nursing college and nobody was going to stop me.

But before I had the chance of doing anything towards my new goal, Dad told me of his plans during one of his visits.

'I've spoken to the Reverend Mother,' he said, 'and you'll be staying on here until you're eighteen to do your matriculation exams. It's all settled.'

I felt my colour rising.

'Then we'll see after your exams what life holds for you,' he continued.

Finally I opened my mouth to find my words.

'Actually, Dad, I have other plans,' I stammered.

Dad's eyebrows raised. He looked puzzled. I stood to my full height and took a deep breath.

'I'm going away to nursing college,' I said. 'Now I'm sixteen this is legal. I want to put something into the war effort.'

For a split second Dad looked as if he was going to argue with me. But I just stared him straight in the eye. Don't even think about stopping me, I thought.

Then he puffed out his cheeks ever so slightly, and narrowed his eyes.

'And how do you suppose you're going to get into this training?' he asked.

My words came out like a torrent. I felt I was fighting for my survival. I couldn't bear the thought of staying in the convent; this was my only chance of escape. So I needed to be clear.

I told him about Maisie, about how I could apply now I was sixteen, about how the course was two years long. I still didn't know much else, except the training was in Birmingham.

To my relief, Dad nodded. 'Give me a small picture of yourself and I'll go and speak to the matron myself,' he said.

So I passed a snapshot of myself to him and he said he'd let me know.

A week later he came back and told me he'd taken the photo and this alone had got me a place. Apparently the Matron had looked at the snap and said, 'Yes, she looks like a fine girl, very pretty.' And I had a place on the course! That's all it seemed to take in those days.

My happiness was dashed though, with more news from home. My lovely friend Margery had died in her sleep after another bout of TB. Dad broke the news in a visit.

'I am sorry, Win,' he said, his eyes shining.

I felt a lump in my throat and told him I had to leave. Then I went to my room and had a little cry. She was like the sister I'd never had and I knew I'd miss her terribly. I even felt a little bit sorry for Olive and wondered how she'd cope.

Chapter Four

Learning to Love

Nursing training was a whole world away from my life at the convent. I very quickly realised I knew nothing whatsoever about nursing or any of the challenges involved. I'd never so much as changed a nappy before, let alone looked after a sick child. But it was my passport to escape, so I was eager to learn.

While training we stayed in a large country house at Wassell Grove, Hagley, Birmingham; basically, it was in the middle of nowhere.

This house was not only our home, but the place where we learned to look after little ones. Everyone was assigned two children for 'adoption'. Mine were two under-fives called Kenny and Mary. Mary was the sweetest, most angelic little thing, whereas Kenny was a little bugger (excuse my language!). I learned how to look after them, wash them, play with them, feed them and, most of all, to love them. This came naturally to me, even if I'd not had very much love myself up until this point.

Many of the kids needing looking after had been placed here while their mothers had gone off to do war work, like working in the munitions factories. Some were placed here almost like boarders and left for the duration of the war. It was a very hard time for families and few could stay together. But everyone just got on with it and made the best of where they were at. Parents weren't allowed to visit their kids in case they upset them and they were difficult to settle again.

There were also kids with various ailments. Once I had to look after a tiny baby with spina bifida. It made me feel so sad to see the helpless little thing, its spine all exposed and just covered with a dressing. In those days these poor mites didn't live for long.

The other nurses were wonderful people and we all became friends. Sister Margaret was our ward sister and it was her job to make sure we were all OK, all in our beds at night and generally doing well.

My first matron was rather nice and settled me in well. But I was soon made aware life was to be different. Once I saw Maisie and rushed over to her to tell her some news or other.

'Maisie! Maisie!' I began breathlessly.

A matron grabbed my arm and tutted. 'We don't refer to each other by our names these days, Winifred,' she snapped. 'Everyone is a "Nurse" here.'

'Sorry,' I babbled. 'I won't forget again.'

I shrugged off her hand and carried on. 'Nurse Maisie!' I cried, trying to continue my conversation . . .

I became friends with many of the girls, but one in particular was a lovely lady called Anna. She'd also joined as a nurse to be independent and get away from home. We loved spending time together. For our evenings out we had to walk two and a half miles over open muddy fields just to catch a bus into Stourbridge, or two miles the other way for a bus to Birmingham on our afternoons off. But we didn't hesitate or complain about it. If we didn't make the effort we'd never leave the building!

And we needed to really, to unwind and relax after hard days at work. As often as we could, if we weren't on night shift, we'd go out ballroom dancing at the local hall.

En route, on the bus, we'd take off our hats and our aprons and stuff them in our bags.

I absolutely loved it. We'd all take our places at the side of the hall and then one by one dance together or sometimes with the boys to all the favourites like Billie Holiday, Frank Sinatra, Johnny Mercer and Nat King Cole. It was just so much fun. For the first time, too, I was mixing with boys and I realised how well I got on with the lads. The young men were the same sort of age as us (late teens) who'd been drafted into the army and were training in the nearby camps before they got sent away on missions abroad. If we weren't dancing, we'd nip to the pub for a lemonade. But it wasn't drinking we were interested in, it was the boys!

I'd always been more comfortable around boys than women. I wasn't sure why. Maybe because out of my two parents I had a slightly better relationship with Dad. Or maybe it was because of my brothers. Even if I didn't see them often, Norman and Ken always wrote to me regularly and I still saw Cliff from time to time. I liked to banter with men, have a laugh, there seemed less bitching and they were more straightforward than women, I always found.

Within a few months of starting another matron, Sister Tutor, took over us and she was just horrible. She'd been in the army and got herself pregnant so had to leave. She obviously had wanted to go back but wasn't allowed and she seemed to take out all her anger and bitterness on us poor girls. She hated me in particular.

I'm not sure why, as I did try my best, but I found it impossible to arrive anywhere on time, there was always something more fun to be doing, especially in the evenings after dancing. We had to be back for lights out by ten o'clock and there I'd be, always a few minutes past.

Sister Tutor used to go ballistic and one evening I felt her full wrath.

'And WHO DO YOU THINK YOU ARE?' she screamed in my face. She was a very tall, imposing-looking lady, but with a plain face – her features had been hardened by years of bitterness, I'd imagine.

'I'm sorry,' I said meekly, scuttling off to my room.

But sorry was not good enough for the likes of Sister Tutor. She started threatening all sorts and woe betide me if I was late again!

Rushing back, night after night, across that field, thick with mud, was no mean feat. We'd all link arms and run as fast as possible down the lonely country lanes, with no lampposts and just us and the cows asleep in the field. Then we had to report to the sister in the main house to say we were home.

But even if I was one minute late, Sister Tutor refused to overlook it – she always seemed to have it in for me. We had two late passes a month and every time I was late Sister would stop my late passes, meaning I'd have to miss a dance.

This eventually reached the stage where they were stopped for six months and, when I was late one more time, in a rage Sister Tutor told me I'd have to be confined to the nurses' home and not stay in the dormitory with the other girls.

My friend Anna and I chewed this decision over after tea.

'I can't stay in all the time!' I complained. 'I'll go mad!'

At the time, I didn't have a regular boyfriend, but we'd started hanging around with the American servicemen outside the pubs in West Hagley. To miss out on this felt like a disaster.

'There must be some way of overcoming this,' said Anna. 'I'm sure we can get one over Sister Tutor.'

I giggled.

'There's nothing I'd like more,' I agreed.

Then we came up with a plan.

The following night, after a hard day's work with Kenny driving me a little crazy and Mary melting my heart like she always did, I planned a big night out even though I was confined to the nurses' home.

After supper, I quickly changed into a dress and then slipped open the bedroom window. I pushed myself out of it and dropped to the ground as soundlessly as possible. Then

I lay flat on my tummy and started wriggling commando-style through the bushes. I couldn't help giggling to myself.

What a thing to be doing, Win! I thought, as I pushed through the leaves on the other side. Leaping to my feet, I ran like lightning across the field to the gate, where Anna was waiting for me, laughing her head off.

'You made it,' she cried.

'I did,' I said, shaking leaves out of my hair. 'Albeit with some extra foliage.'

Anna had two bikes with her, borrowed from the nearby stables. It was part of our plan on how to get home even quicker that evening. I don't think either of us could believe our plan had worked and we set off. That evening of dancing and chatting to boys was one of the best ever. I suppose all stolen apples taste the sweetest and this evening was no exception.

Back at the bus stop, we picked up our bikes where we'd hidden them at the roadside and rode back as fast as possible.

I still had to get back in undetected though! Retracing my tummy-wiggling technique, I slid back in through the window and just made it in time to undress, ruffle my hair and collapse under the bedclothes when I heard a knock at the door.

Feigning a tired voice, I said, 'Come in!' blinking like a blind woman.

'Everything all right, Nurse?' asked Sister Margaret in the half-light. It was her job to check we were all in our beds.

'Yes,' I yawned as innocently as possible, scratching my head. 'I'd just dropped off, actually.'

'Good,' she said, before turning on her heel.

Bless her, I thought. She must have known something was awry, but she didn't breathe a word.

For a while I was happy just to chat to all the boys, never having one particular boyfriend, when one day, someone came into my life who changed everything. His name was George Wheeler.

Tall, with dark shiny hair and shiny brown eyes to match, I liked the look of him from the beginning. He was just so handsome.

He bought me a lemonade and we got talking. Softly spoken and really rather gentle, I thought he had a lovely manner. He was the first boy I ever took real notice of. He was in the RAF, training after leaving his job in a printing shop.

'I can't wait to get up in the air,' he enthused. 'Imagine! Flying on top of the world.'

His enthusiasm was infectious. I knew I'd met a man with real spirit, but also a gentle kindness.

After our dance, he walked me to the bus stop. 'Can I see you again, Win?' he asked, taking my hand. He felt so warm.

I nodded. I wasn't sure one way or another, but I was fond of him already so I'd see where it led.

The next few times I saw George, we started talking and didn't stop all evening again. Then at the end of one night, as the dance finished he picked up the microphone and began singing into it. Everyone fell into a hushed silence as he looked up and searched for my face. Once he spotted me, he gazed at me as he sang so beautifully you could almost feel everyone's heart melt. He certainly melted mine in that instant.

I'd no idea he possessed such a powerful voice either.

Afterwards everyone clapped, but George just handed back the microphone shyly and came and stood by my side.

I squeezed his hand. 'You've got a lovely voice,' I whispered.

He didn't reply, but just pecked me on the cheek.

We wandered back to the bus stop, hand in hand, gazing at the stars again.

'I really hate saying goodbye to you, Win,' he said. 'I think I'm in love with you.'

Hearing those words sent such a wonderful warm feeling across my very being, I cannot tell you. Nobody, not ever, had said that to me before.

'I love you,' he repeated, as if I hadn't heard right the first time.

He smiled, his eyes crinkling in the corners a little.

I felt myself welling up a little, but took a deep breath to compose myself. And I knew then, in that moment, there was nobody in the world I loved more than him too.

'I love you too!' I cried.

We had a little kiss, as if sealing our thoughts together. And from that moment on, we vowed to spend as much time as possible together.

So we did. Every free night for us both we'd meet and spend hours together, talking, kissing, holding hands . . . it was all enough just to be sat by this man's side for me. I couldn't believe how lucky I was. And best of all, he felt just as lucky to have me as well.

George was going to have to go away for more training soon. He couldn't say much about this work, but I soon learned he was taking a different path to some of his friends. They were training to work on the ground, whereas George was fulfilling his ambition to go up in the air. His dark eyes shone even brighter as he gazed at the night sky to tell me about it.

'Just imagine how it will feel!' he said, pointing to the stars, which seemed to be twinkling even brighter that evening, just for us. 'I'll be up there soon, seeing the world.'

I nodded. We had more in common than I'd ever imagined.

'I'd like to see the world too,' I grinned. 'In fact I rather like the idea of joining the army. Go abroad. Get away from it all.'

George did a double take at me. 'Really, Win?' he said. 'The army?'

'Yes,' I said, sitting down on a grassy bank by the bus stop. I hugged my knees as I warmed to the idea. I'd thought of the army a few times, but never spoke of my dreams out loud. I was a very private person and usually kept my thoughts to myself. But with George it was different. Everything was different.

'I love the idea of travelling everywhere, free as a bird. Seeing new countries, other cultures, how other people

47

live. I'd love to serve my country too. Not just with boring old nursing but with the women's army. It would be so exciting!'

I thought of the Clent Hills, around three miles away, which could clearly be seen from the window at the nursing house. They looked like mountains to me and every shift I'd find myself staring out of the window and thinking, one day I'll go far, far beyond them.

George smiled, but he also shook his head. 'Oh, Win, what a dreamer you are,' he said. 'I love your sense of adventure but I'm not sure women should be in the army. It doesn't seem right! The army is a man's job.'

George laughed and pulled me closer to him. 'You're an amazing woman though,' he said. I half-laughed, feeling vaguely embarrassed now about telling him.

He took my hand. 'One thing though, whatever happens, I hope all our dreams come true,' he said. His face lit up as the bus headlights flooded our vision.

My heart always sank when the bus arrived. It meant bursting my bubble and saying goodbye to George.

We didn't usually talk about dreams. It was an unspoken thing that they were out of bounds. No one dared at this time. It was wartime and nobody could take for granted what would happen the following day, let alone the following week, month . . . or year. The future was a big unknown, a big void and nobody dared think otherwise.

'Until next time,' he said, giving me a lingering kiss on the lips. Like always, I sat in my seat and pressed my face into the bus window. We waved and waved until George grew smaller and disappeared. Then I sank into my seat to think about what a lovely evening I'd had, and start counting down the hours until our next one.

Chapter Five

Letters Straight from the Heart

Life as a nurse was a huge eye-opener for me. One of my first postings was at Lordswood Road Maternity Hospital. Although I'd dealt with a few babies by now, I'd never seen one delivered and felt it to be an important part of my training.

I clearly remember the shock of seeing some of the ladies giving birth. During one particular labour the poor woman was suffering agonising pain as she was having a long breach delivery. Contorted in pain, she screamed and moaned like an animal, writhing on the bed as doctors watched on, waiting to see how far it went.

It was so awful to watch, as doctors just gazed at her, looking at their watches. I found myself gripping the end of the bedstead, willing it to be over for her.

On this occasion, a doctor pointed at me and a nurse came over.

'Nurse Win, you have to leave,' she said firmly. She took my elbow and led me out of the room. I felt anger rising in my chest.

'Why are you doing this to me?' I hissed. 'What have I done?'

The nurse looked vaguely amused as I clearly had no idea. 'Your face is so pale the doctor thought you'd pass out,' she laughed.

He was right. I was upset to see a woman suffering in such a way. But at the same time I wanted to stay put and do my job properly.

When George had to go away and do some training we always wrote to each other, every single day if we could. I loved his funny letters, always telling me about what he was up to (within reason, as the letters were censored) and asking me about my day.

I wrote about what I'd seen or heard on the ward, what the kids were up to, and how awful Sister Tutor was being. For both of us we'd found someone to confide in as well as laugh with.

'You wouldn't believe what happened,' George said in one letter. 'One of my squad saw me with you last week and asked what I'd been doing with a schoolgirl. Oh, Win, it's because you look so very young still. But actually I soon set them straight. You're very much a woman to me . . .'

In turn, I replied telling him of all the gory things I had to see during the day. 'These poor women really do suffer,' I penned.

'Does it put you off the idea of having a baby one day?' George responded in his next letter.

'Not at all,' I replied. 'It's hard watching other people but I am sure it's not as bad as it seems . . .'

Although babies still seemed like a long way off, some-times I caught myself dreaming about something before that. Marriage to George. For some reason I just knew we would be married one day. If only this blessed war was over!

Although I witnessed some shocking things like women in agony, we nurses did manage to find a laugh when we could on the wards.

One prank all the girls liked playing was telling someone the matron wanted to see them, and urgently! This meant you'd have to run around frantically for a few minutes, making up a new butterfly cap, changing your apron and making sure you looked spick and span before running to the matron's door.

On one occasion I was just about to knock, when someone tapped me on the shoulder.

'It's just a joke,' a nurse whispered, dissolving into giggles.

Another time I woke up in the middle of the night to answer the call of nature. As I padded down the corridor, half asleep, a passing nurse on night duty gasped. 'Win! Do you know what the time is? You'd better get a chivvy on or you'll be late for the start of your shift!' she chided.

Within a millisecond I'd gone from half asleep to wide awake, heart racing. Oh goodness, I couldn't afford to be late for the start of the day too. Sister Tutor really would kill me!

'Is it that time already?' I cried. It was still dark outside, but most mornings were dark when we began. 'Oh damn.'

Mum's Army

I rushed to my room, barely catching my breath as I threw on my uniform, my fingers as nimbly as possible folding my butterfly hat (they were always tricky and fiddly, really quite hellish to put together), then I whizzed back to join the others.

As they spotted me, rushing towards them, fixing my apron on my back as I ran, I heard the tell-tale sniggers.

'What you doing here, Win?' said one innocently, glancing at her watch. 'It's only . . . ooh . . . three a.m.'

I took a second and then laughed back too. Although it was annoying, you could only join in. I felt a fool, but I knew it'd be someone else's turn the next day.

Although it would have been very much frowned upon due to rationing, sometimes a nurse or two would come up with the idea of a midnight feast.

These were always nerve-wracking occasions, as we'd be in big trouble if the matron found out, but I was always game.

One time, one of the girls, Nurse Margaret, cooked up some bacon and chips and we all arranged cushions on the floor of the sitting room. A fair few girls trooped down and we sat around, talking in hushed whispers and quickly eating the food.

Our sitting room overlooked a wide drive and we all gazed across at the night sky through the shutters.

'You know,' said one nurse, her mouth full of bacon, 'I've heard a few prisoners from a POW camp nearby have escaped!'

'I hope the smell of bacon doesn't lure them to us,' laughed Margaret.

Just as she said this, we heard a tap-tap on the window shutters. We all stopped chewing in unison and gasped.

'What the blazes was that?' gasped one of the girls.

With wide eyes in the dim of the room, Margaret took charge. 'Right, everyone back to bed,' she ordered. 'Win, you clear up and we'll investigate.'

I wasn't too sure I wanted to, but leaped to my feet and collected the greasy plates left behind as the nurses dashed back to their beds.

The tapping noise continued as I bustled into the kitchen with the stack of dishes.

'Margaret,' I whispered. 'What is it?'

She looked pale. 'I don't know.'

She helped put the plates in the sink and we quickly washed them so Matron wouldn't suspect anything. Then we tiptoed back upstairs to a small balcony at the front of the house. Even from upstairs we could hear this insistent tapping. My mind was racing. Perhaps it really was a burglar, or someone trying to get in! Margaret, bless her, bravely opened the window and stepped outside, with me looking over her shoulder.

Gingerly we peered down below.

But instead of seeing any man we clapped eyes on big black and white beasts, all jostling for position and mooing softly.

'Looks like our prisoners of war are actually a bunch of cows,' chuckled Margaret. Six stray cows had wandered from the farm down the road.

My laughter soon vanished though when Margaret asked

me to join in chasing them away. I was terrified they'd step on my feet or try and get in the house.

After being trained as a wireless operator at Halfpenny Green, George was set to be posted to Mildenhall in Suffolk, and from there he'd be sent on his first bombing assignment. His role was to be sat in a cramped space just above the fuse-lage of the bomb bay of the plane where he'd be listening for instructions, like weather updates or changes in tactics. I was so proud of him. It was a job for a clever, quick fellow, who could handle the pressure.

I knew he was facing a dangerous job though, there was no doubt about that. He'd be flying in Lancaster bombers to Germany on air-raid missions. I shut out the worries whirl-ing in my mind as much as possible. There was no point in even thinking of the worst. There was nothing either of us could do to change it.

George was always upbeat and planning our next meet-ings.

'Before I go away, Win,' he said. 'I'd like you to meet Mum and Dad.'

I couldn't help but feel butterflies. To me, if a man introduces you to his parents it means he's serious. I already knew we were but this was further proof of his commit-ment to me.

'I'd love to,' I said.

They lived in Morecambe and were close to George. They were probably especially fond of him as they'd already lost their eldest son, George's brother. He'd died in his late teens of a chest infection, before he'd achieved his ambition of training to be a priest. It sounded like a terrible tragedy and my heart went out to them.

George told me all about it on one of our long walks. A few times we went from Stourbridge to Pedmore, just taking in the green hills and country lanes and nattering non-stop about our lives.

One day, while I was visiting Dad at home, I got a telegram. I was so thrilled to see it was from George.

'You're welcome. STOP. To come and stay. STOP. How about next Wednesday. STOP. I'll meet you in Birmingham Snow Hill. STOP.'

I was so excited. Dad had seen a telegram arrive but didn't know what it was about. I knew it was time to ask him.

'Dad, I am going to Morecambe,' I said, with my usual forthrightness. 'It's to stay with a boy I've met and his family.'

Dad gave me a sideways look up from his paper. Olive, of course, always listening and poking her nose in when it wasn't wanted, also glanced up.

'Oh, so that's what the telegram was about,' Dad began.

'Yes, that's what it was about,' I said. 'And I'd like to go.'

Dad sucked in his lips as he mulled it over, but before he even spoke, Olive was jumping in.

'No!' she said loudly to Dad. 'She's not going! You can't let her!'

It was all I could do to stop myself from screaming 'Shut up!' to her. I clenched a fist behind my back. I just wished she'd keep her nose out of my business.

'I *am* going, Dad,' I said, levelly. 'It's only for four days.'

'No,' replied Olive, still not looking at me but at Dad. 'She's to stay here. We can't let her go.'

Finally Dad spoke. 'OK,' he said, wearily. 'Just behave yourself.'

I think he just wanted to avoid a row with me. But also I think he was sympathetic on some level about my desire to be with this man. He understood the war was on. He knew George would be going away to fight.

I was thrilled. Four whole days with my beloved George. What absolute bliss! I ran upstairs to start packing and deciding what clothes to take.

The day I set off in 1943, I was almost quaking with nerves and excitement. I longed to make a good impression with his parents.

As we'd arranged, I met him at Birmingham Snow Hill station. He looked as handsome as ever as he met me on the platform, wrapping me in his usual bear hug. He took my case and then my hand, firmly, and we slipped onto the train together.

We jumped on a bus when we got to Morecambe. Chatting all the way, I suddenly felt nervous as we pulled up near his parents' house. It was a flat, in part of a bigger house. So much of Morecambe had been bombed by then, people were having to live in smaller places.

I started fussing with my hair, but George took my hand and smiled at me.

'You look perfect in every way, Win,' he said. 'They will love you as much as I do.'

His mother greeted me at the door with a warm hug.

George was right, I couldn't have been made more welcome.

The next few days passed all too quickly in a blur of delicious meals, lovely walks by the sea and deep conversations. On the Sunday we all went to church for Mass. Whenever I was with George I felt like I was existing in a lovely bubble, and I didn't want it to end.

On our last day we went for a long walk on the wind-swept beach. Even when the skies were grey, it looked beautiful to me. The beach was vast and full of shingle and we laughed as we struggled to walk on it. George directed us, making sure we could manage on the easy bits. I just felt so protected by him. So loved and cared for.

'You make me so very, very happy,' I said to him.

As it is when you're enjoying yourself so very much, time sped past all too quickly. For some reason I knew I'd treasure those few days we had together whatever happened.

And that was it during the war, you never knew what would happen. He never said it aloud, but I had a horrible feeling that George believed he wouldn't be coming back.

Of course, we never spoke about this. We took each day as it came.

I said a warm goodbye to his parents. They looked quite teary as they said goodbye, as if waving off a much-loved relative.

'See you soon,' promised his mum, squeezing my hands firmly. And I genuinely hoped I would.

They were a lovely family. One day, I dared myself to think, perhaps George and I would have a family like this.

Mum's Army

George saw me to the bus stop so I could get back to Birmingham.

He looked me deeply in the eyes. 'I will write to you every single time I land safely after each mission,' he said. 'I can't write about where I'm going, but I promise I will write about when I return.'

I nodded. We were both so choked with emotion, I couldn't find my words.

Once again, I found myself sitting on a bus, looking through the glass, not wanting to tear my eyes away from my lovely George. We'd had nine months together by now. And all I longed for was more.

'Until next time . . . goodbye, George,' I mouthed through the window, waving furiously.

He carried on waving, one hand in his pocket, the other held high. And when he couldn't see my hand anymore he stood still, watching my bus, until finally we turned a corner and he was gone.

I breathed out a long sigh, clasping my hands in the way I'd just held George's, and closed my eyes. I just wanted this damned war to be over. Over. Then we could get on with our lives. Until then, I'd just have to be patient, something I wasn't too good at. But I was sure I'd manage it. For me and George it was worth it.

Along with waiting for letters from George, I also regularly received them from my brother Norman, who was in the Coldstream Guards and was stationed abroad. He got engaged to a lovely girl, Julie, just before he went. I was so happy for him. It looked like he'd found happiness at last. We'd always kept in touch by letter throughout the years. But it was sporadic as the postal system wasn't very good at all.

One time I got only one letter in two years and it was to let me know he'd been taken prisoner in Tobruk in North Africa. The Italians had captured him and then handed him over to the Germans. Always a plucky character, Norman managed to escape in 1941 and fled to live with a local family somewhere in Germany where he was being held.

After a few days though, he was found. As part of his punishment he was made to stand and watch as each family member who had fed and sheltered him so kindly for those few days was shot dead in front of him. It was a terrible trauma I think he never ever could recover from.

Meanwhile Ken had joined the signals corps and wherever he was he always wrote me a postcard. I treasured all of them.

Thankfully I had my busy work to take my mind off all the worries for my brothers and George. I was dog-tired by the end of each day and usually fell asleep as soon as my head hit the pillow. But beforehand, I loved seeing familiar blue envelopes with the RAF emblem waiting for me in my room.

George kept to his word and sent me letters whenever he could, usually every single evening.

'Back safe,' he'd say, before launching into something about the countryside he'd seen or what he'd had to eat. Obviously he was censored and could tell me nothing about each mission until afterwards.

We wrote long notes to each other. I'd make sure I was alone before ripping his open, savouring every word. I loved the way letters were so personal. I'd trace his words penned in his swirly neat handwriting, imagining him bent over a desk or resting on his knee after the end of a hard day, scribbling away, thinking of me.

Sometimes he wrote beautiful poetry. He was very observant and would notice the natural world around him . . . wildlife, the shape of the trees, the colour of the grass, the majesty of a hill, anything really. I'd have quite blushed if he'd said them to my face. But actually that was the thing about George. Even though he was brave enough to wish to fly in the air, he was a sensitive soul beneath it all. He always ended his letters by saying how much he loved me.

Once he sketched a pencil drawing of different styles of house. 'One day when peace arrives I hope to live somewhere like this with you . . . choose which one you'd like to live in and send it back to me,' he wrote.

I smiled, holding the letter to me as I lay back on my bed. I picked a pretty-fronted plain bungalow with square windows and a smart front door, one of his sketches.

'This is the one!' I wrote, circling his drawing. 'Would make us a perfect home!'

I couldn't have imagined anything nicer. Me and George, living in our bungalow. I knew we'd marry at the end of the war. In my heart I just knew it.

The war could take away so much but never our dreams.

* * *

Around 1943, I heard the devastating news that Auntie Annie's sweet shop had been destroyed by a bomb. It was all so sad. She'd set everything up so her family could be provided for. She wanted to give the shop to one of her children and then she had houses for the other two. They were investments for the future to give them the best start in life. But it didn't work out quite like that. After the sweet shop had gone, Uncle Percy moved in with Kitty to one of the houses saved for their daughter.

The senselessness of war hit me again then. Poor Auntie Annie, who'd worked so hard to see all her family were provided for, had put in all that effort for nothing.

After about six months apart, I had a whole library of letters from George. They were always a joy to open. Sometimes I had to wait a few days for his next one, but without fail I'd get one. I kept them all together in a neat bundle and put them in my bedside drawer.

Then one day George sent me a picture of himself wearing his civvy clothes. Boy, did he look handsome in it. His hair was neatly swept back, he wasn't smiling, but he looked so lovely still. His defined jawline, his beautiful eyes, all looked as if they belonged to a movie star.

I very proudly stuck his picture up on my wall and all the girls commented on it.

'He's a good-looking chap,' one said.

'You're a lucky one,' sighed another.

It always made me beam from ear to ear. 'That's my George,' I replied.

George had accompanied it with a letter.

'All the lads have had to have a photo taken of themselves wearing civvies. It's for ID purposes. If we get shot down and end up in enemy hands we can claim to be civilians and evade capture.'

Some of the aircrew had been taught German in case of ending up behind enemy lines but in George's case he didn't have time. He was just quickly trained to do his job and that was it, he was sent up into the skies to get his job done.

I was so proud of him. I was sure he must've been afraid but he didn't show it. He just embraced this new life and really rose to the challenge. Life in the RAF did seem rather exciting. It made me think about army life again, but I pushed the thought from my mind. I already had a decent job and, besides, I knew I was in an exemption occupation now. Nurses were needed as part of the war effort.

I didn't know when George would be back on leave, and neither did he, but I couldn't wait all the same.

Christmas came and went and with rationing and working my shifts it was pretty uneventful. As we saw in 1944, I really hoped a new future was around the corner. I knew the war was dragging on and on but there were signs of possible surrenders. We could all just live in hope.

George was often away on missions over Stuttgart now. It was part of a strategic Allied air offensive against the Germans. The city had a big industrial scene, with major rail links to southwestern Germany, military bases and car manufacturing . . . a city rather like Coventry in that respect. It was a prime target and I never heard how the raids went.

Nothing was reported at the time and I was just grateful to hear from George when he returned.

But in July, I didn't get a letter from George for a few days. At the end of each shift I went to my room and found nothing.

'Come on, George, where are you?' I said to myself, staring at my ceiling in bed.

I didn't like to think of him thousands of feet in the air, tackling enemy gunfire, but now my imagination was running a little wild. I squeezed my eyes shut to close out the thoughts. All I could do was get up, do my job, come back to my room, hope and wait.

I tried not to worry. But when the days dragged into a week, then ten days, then two weeks, I started to fear the worst.

Chapter Six

Into the Darkness

In August 1944 an envelope with a Morecambe postmark arrived with unfamiliar handwriting scrawled on it. I didn't think much about who it was from and ripped it open to look before I had a chance to think too deeply.

Scanning the short note, two words leaped out as my hands started trembling: 'Missing' and George's mum's signature.

I read it again and again to make sure I wasn't imagining it. My heart was beating so fast I thought it would split my chest open.

'I've had word George is missing in action. His last mission was on the evening of July 24th/25th and he was flying home. I'm so sorry . . .' his mum had written. It was short, to the point, full of pain. Nobody knew what had happened to George. She had no further information to give. He was just listed by the RAF as officially missing. To begin with, I took a few seconds to digest it. Then it felt as if a tidal wave of utter horror and what I can only describe as pure grief swept over me.

No, I thought. No, no, no, noooo . . .

I just couldn't believe it. Not George. Not my George.

I felt wet drops streaming off my chin as I realised my face was running like a tap. The pain was indescribable. I threw my face onto a pillow and allowed my sobs out. I just wanted to curl up and disappear. This was awful. Just too, too awful. Then Anna popped her head in to see if I was going out dancing that evening.

'Win?' she said.

She took one look at my puffy face, and her eye fell on the letter I was still clutching.

'Aw, Win,' she said. 'Not George? I am so, so sorry.'

She sat down next to me, slid her arm around my shoulder and said nothing. After all, what was there to say?

I cried myself to sleep and when I woke up, I was still in tears.

The next few weeks passed in a blur. I didn't know what to do. 'Missing' is such a terrible word. Did it mean he'd been captured? Could he still be alive? I tried to shake this thought. He couldn't be. It didn't mean that. I couldn't let myself go down that road.

I wanted so badly to ring his mum, talk to her, share the pain, but somehow I knew this would be upsetting for her. She'd already lost one son, now she'd lost both of them. They were such lovely parents; it was a terrible, terrible thing. Even then, I knew their lives would be totally shattered by the loss of both their sons, by this terribly unjust loss, whereas for me, I was young and would one day possibly recover. I understood that even in my darkest hour, although I couldn't ever imagine how.

I walked like a ghost around the wards for the next few weeks. Just a shell of a person. I didn't want to eat, or sleep, or do anything. I simply couldn't believe the man I loved had gone.

Then I sat down and wrote his mum a letter, telling her how sorry I was.

'He was a very special person,' I said. Somehow though, words of comfort seemed so meaningless.

She replied with a warm response, so I wrote again, asking her what she thought had happened and whether we could find any more news. What had become of George?

I suppose in this next letter she saw my pain very clearly.

'You can't go on like this, Winifred,' she wrote. 'It will make things too painful for you. We are going to have to accept he has gone, as hard as this is.'

I cried so much. I knew she was right. I knew I'd go mad if I didn't try and think past this. I felt so sorry for her and his father too. This awful war! It all felt very pointless indeed right then. Taking these lovely young men, in their prime, and just shedding their blood.

Everyone tiptoed around me trying to make me feel better. But nothing did. I felt so isolated, so alone. I never, ever dreamed this could happen. I knew it was a possibility, but now for some reason it had occurred, I just felt totally unprepared. I couldn't face going dancing or anywhere. I managed somehow to get through my days at work and then went straight to bed. Even just getting through the day without crying was hard. I never knew grief could be so profoundly tiring, but even in bed I couldn't sleep. There was no escape from this pain in my heart and the only way to deal with it was to learn to live with it. Just like so many others had to.

One evening, one of the nurses knocked on my door.

'Come on, Win!' she cried. 'You never come out anymore! You can't stay in for the rest of your life.'

'I can,' I said. I felt so drained. Drained of life now. What was the point?

Some more nurses stuck their head around the door.

'Oh, Win!' said one. 'Your pilot boy will be dead. He'll have been shot down. He's at the bottom of the sea now, with the fish! Just put it to the back of your mind and come out!'

I felt anger welling up now. 'You just dare say that again to me!' I cried, turning my head into my pillow. 'Just leave me alone.'

I burst into tears, not knowing what to do with myself. It was all such a mess. I didn't even know what had happened to George. It felt as if my future had been ripped away from me and I didn't even understand why. If I'd known then that it would take me another fifty years before I'd find out the truth as to what had happened, I think it would've killed me too.

The months didn't seem to do anything to ease the pain. But I grew accustomed to living with it: the ball of pain in my stomach, the tears always ready behind my eyes. The world felt like a different place now. Empty.

Mum's Army

I wasn't interested in any other boys when I did finally go dancing again. I just felt hollow and went through the motions, a smile plastered on my face like a mask.

'Getting on with it' was the phrase in those days. And I suppose after sort of losing my parents at a young age, I'd learned independence to some extent.

But I knew I'd miss George forever, even if I also knew I had to carry on living. So each morning I just put one foot in front of the other and plodded on. What choice did I have?

Soon afterwards though, there was even less peace when I made my way down to the ward and found it empty of nurses and with a harassed-looking matron watching the clock.

'Good,' she said, when I arrived along with another nurse, Jane. 'At least we have you two. Now all the other nurses have come down with thrush . . . every single one, so it will be all hands to the pump today for you.'

All the others had been hospitalised for treatment and we literally had to do everything ourselves.

'You two will have to work jolly hard,' barked the matron at us. And, boy, was she right. We were rushing round like bluebottles all day long, just trying to keep up.

It was a nightmare but somehow we got through it. That evening, we sat down, exhausted, to eat our evening meal. I quite liked the stew and dumplings but when the next course arrived, I couldn't help but push it aside. It was rice pudding, and looked like a glutinous pile of something unmentionable.

'No thank you,' I said, as it was placed in front of me.

Matron spotted my refusal, something she deeply disapproved of. 'You'll eat it and be grateful,' she snapped. 'There's a war on, remember.'

That was a favourite phrase always being banded around then. 'There's a war on.' It seemed to mean you always had to do something you didn't want to.

If I do eat it they'll regret it, I thought to myself, as I resentfully swilled my spoon around the bowl. With the matron's sharp eye on me I slowly lifted it to my mouth and shuddered. The feeling of the creamy, fatty milk in my mouth truly made me want to vomit.

I managed a few mouthfuls and when she wasn't looking ditched the rest.

That evening both myself and the other nurse began to feel rather like we had the flu. Our temperatures were sky-high and we both felt sick. We tossed and turned in bed, until the matron called a doctor to us.

'You both have yellow jaundice,' he declared. 'You'll need a spell in hospital, bed-bound.'

Yellow jaundice is a contagious liver disease. The doctor prescribed medicines and told us to avoid all fatty foods, and that was when the rice pudding sprang to mind. I had yet another reason for avoiding it then.

While in bed, someone was playing a wireless from somewhere and I kept hearing Vera Lynn singing her heart out. She was the Forces' sweetheart and everyone loved her. But being bed-bound and forced to listen to repeat playings of 'We'll Meet Again' was a step too far. It was maddening and I longed to clamp a pillow around my ears. Even today when I hear Vera Lynn sing, I am somehow transported back to that terrible time and that bed.

While I lay recovering in my hospital bed, Dad came to see me. Well, I thought he was coming to see me, but actually he just had some news to relay.

'I'm marrying Olive,' he said simply, 'and I'd like you and Cliff to attend the wedding.'

I barely managed to hide my reaction of indifference and when I winced slightly, pretended it was in pain.

'OK,' I said, shifting my position in the bed.

I couldn't have cared less, as I knew how little she cared for us.

The ceremony was held in a church in the Cadbury area. By now Cliff was a cheeky sixteen-year-old and made his feelings very clear about going to his dad's wedding.

As we sat next to each other on the pews, he turned to me and loudly offered me a piece of chocolate.

'Do you want some, Win?' he asked, munching loudly.

'Shhhh, Cliff!' I said, horrified. 'We're in a church!'

'I don't care,' replied Cliff, shrugging his shoulders.

I managed to hush him up long enough to see the ceremony through. We watched as Olive pledged to be Dad's wife and dutifully clapped as they walked back down the aisle as newly-weds.

As we followed them out of the church, Cliff said a little too loudly, 'What are you going to call her?'

'Auntie Olive, I suppose,' I replied.

'I'm not!' retorted Cliff. 'She's no auntie to me!' Again, a little too loudly.

Once we got to the reception, held in one of the Cadbury social clubs, Dad pointed at myself and Cliff and mouthed: 'Come here, you two.'

Wagging his finger at us, he said, 'You'll call my wife "Auntie Olive", you hear?'

We both nodded, but afterwards Cliff just shrugged and went off to look for some sausage rolls.

Of course, George was never far from my mind. Not knowing what had happened to him was terrible. But I stopped allowing myself to imagine one minute that he'd been found in a prisoner of war camp, and the next minute standing at his grave. I just had to accept he was gone and that was that. All I could do was try my best to shut out these images and focus on the day. Just get through the day.

I remembered all of our conversations, sometimes going over them in my head, just so I wouldn't forget. Every moment we had spent together felt so precious now. I recalled our conversation about the army too.

'It's not for women!' he'd teased affectionately.

And I'd laughed back. But actually I still wanted, more than ever now, to escape over those Clent Hills and see the world. I wanted to get away.

One day I brought up the subject with Dad. I'd need his permission if I joined up before the age of twenty-one.

His face dropped immediately.

'Absolutely completely not,' he said firmly. 'I will never give permission for any daughter of mine to sign up.'

I sighed. This time I knew I couldn't defy him. I needed his signature and that was that. It meant I'd be forced to wait until I was twenty-one. I said nothing, and just hoped the years would fly by. I knew by now I'd never make a natural nurse, and another life for me was beckoning for sure.

Work kept me busy and drama was never far away, especially as far as Sister Tutor was concerned. Her new catchphrase at the time to someone who hadn't done something as she liked was to yell: 'You're stark staring raving mad!' It drove me almost mad just to listen to it!

Even though I'd proven myself to be a decent nurse, she never let me be. One day a young sister called Edith was caught shoplifting in the town. She'd been a friend to me and was a lovely quiet sort. I could only imagine she had a compulsion to steal from being unhappy deep down, but she never mentioned anything to me.

Anyway, she was caught red-handed and arrested. Back at the house, it was a scandal, with everyone muttering about it.

Sister Tutor was obviously in full form that night as her mood seemed more foul than ever. It was a Saturday night and as I arrived back from an evening out in the pub, she was standing at the top of the staircase, looking down at me, her nostrils quivering.

As I looked up she said at the top of her voice, 'You, Winifred. You were with Edith when this happened, weren't you?'

73

I looked at her as if she was mad. But she carried on. 'Weren't you?' she snapped.

I opened my mouth to speak, but another nurse, a lovely lady called Nurse Nichols, ushered me out of the room and to bed.

I felt so confused. What was Tutor on about this time? It was also very bad form indeed to be accusing me in front of people like that. How dare she! I went to bed, but tossed and turned, unable to sleep. It was such an unhappy time really.

The next morning, Nurse Nichols knocked on my door. She came in and looked at me seriously. 'I want you to write a letter to the Nursing Body and make an official complaint about Tutor,' she said, briskly. 'About what she said to you. It was very wrong of her to accuse you like that.'

I nodded. I wasn't usually one to cause a fuss but did as she told me.

A few days later I was summoned to the Nursing Association offices and officially interviewed. They asked me a few questions about Sister Tutor, all nodding and listening intently as I told the truth. Then I was thanked for my time and sent back.

Soon after, I heard Sister Tutor was now 'working her notice'. I could barely catch my breath.

'Wow,' said Anna. 'The old bitch is going thanks to you!'

I couldn't quite believe it. She'd been so horrid and now it was over. I didn't feel in the least bit sorry for her.

It wasn't long afterwards I knew it was time to move on from Hagley. I needed a fresh start, so I applied for a job as staff nurse at a hospital in Prescot, Liverpool. I was sad to be leaving the house in the country, but also very ready for pastures new. It was time to move on with my life.

As I packed up my things, I carefully placed George's bundle of letters in my suitcase. I couldn't bear to be apart from them. They were all I had left.

I said goodbye to the girls, vowing to keep in touch, and set off again. In many ways I was at my happiest when I was on the move.

It was around this time the idea of going into the army appealed again. It would mean constant moving, travel, excitement, adventures. But nothing could stop me now. I made a few enquires but was told as I was in a reserved occupation they still couldn't let me join HM forces.

So I settled down to hospital life in Liverpool, but it was hard going. This hospital was even stricter than my last place. It was enormous, with a massive long ward with a matron station overseeing everything and everyone in the middle.

As always, I quickly made friends and grew close to one in particular, a cheery nurse called Pat. She showed me the ropes to make things easier.

'It's hard graft in this place,' she said.

'What time do we have to be back for bed?' I asked.

'Nine-thirty,' she said.

I gasped. That was even earlier than the last place. It seemed such a shame as Liverpool was a bustling city, full of dancehalls and bands of an evening. We'd barely have time to get there before we had to come home again!

I still stuck a smile on my face though. 'Well, I'm sure there are ways to still have fun,' I said.

Try as I might though, I couldn't ever seem to get things right. One evening I was on night shift and tried to smooth things over with the matron who had clearly taken a dislike to me. Although this time it wasn't me, it was just about everyone.

'I'll make tea,' I brightly volunteered this particularly busy night.

I went and cheerfully made six cups to take back onto the ward. There was nothing a cuppa couldn't sort out.

I placed them carefully on a tray and then began walking down the ward, balancing them carefully. But as I walked down the long, long ward, I heard the sister's voice boom out.

'Mind that lump of wax!' she cried.

Wax was used to polish the floor so you could practically see your face in it (another job I detested). But with the tray in front I could barely see where I was putting my feet, let alone any foreign objects, and before I could even pause, I felt something hard, slightly gooey and very, very slippery beneath my sole.

'Ooooomph . . .'

In the split second I was sailing through the air, I flung the tray as hard as I could away from me, so I wasn't scalded.

The shattering noise of splintering porcelain and the metal tray slamming into the floor was enough to wake the dead.

'Phhhhhhhhhilllllllippps!' Matron managed to scream my name in such a way that conveyed horror, anger and slight concern all at the same time.

'Sorry, Matron,' I mumbled as I tried to scramble to my feet.

I found myself miserably mopping the floor to add to my list of duties that evening.

The hours we worked were long and hard. I fell ill a few times with sinus problems or suffered from chilblains in the cold. Sometimes the chilblains grew so bad they'd travel up my arms and legs but I was rarely allowed time off.

I found some of the patients' cases so disturbing too. Part of the area the hospital covered was very deprived and so we saw the side of life that often went unnoticed.

Once I found a poor young woman sitting on her bed, waiting for her bed bath, looking cowed as a frightened animal. She'd been admitted suffering from scurvy, a disease caused by lack of vitamin C. It caused lethargy, depression, spots and neurological problems. The disease was first detected in sailors who didn't get enough fresh fruit and vegetables on ships but it wasn't until 1932 the actual link with vitamin C was made. It felt like a travesty, people still suffering from this in our modern age.

As I gently moved her pillow I also noticed little white dots moving busily in her hair. She was crawling with lice. How she'd got into such a state I never knew, but in a way it wasn't surprising. Liverpool was full of slum housing at this time. There was poverty like I'd never seen before.

Another lady had cancer and was covered with sores on her legs as it ate its way through her body. She'd cry and scream all night, however many painkillers we administered never being enough. Sometimes all this human suffering was as much as I could bear. Deep down I didn't like nursing much at all. I struggled with the horror, and found the work laborious at times. After years in a convent I was fed up of being stuck in the same place day in and day out. My thirst for adventure and the longing to escape, far from expiring, was growing stronger.

Chapter Seven

Picking up Pieces

Then, on 8 May 1945, everything changed again. The Allied forces accepted the unconditional surrender of Germany and peace was declared. And the news of this filtered down through the wireless, now switched on near the sister's station. Everything and everyone seemed to pause as Churchill's voice declaring peace rang out: 'We may allow ourselves a brief period of rejoicing . . .' Of course, Japan hadn't surrendered yet, but to know the German fight was over was enough for now. It was incredible.

'The war is over!' everyone chanted to one another, as people paused to hug one another in the corridors. The joy and excitement was infectious. Whoever anybody had lost or whatever you'd suffered, it was impossible to be anything but overwhelmed with happiness.

'I can't believe it!' all the girls kept repeating with smiles on their faces.

Friends or strangers who passed each other in the corridors broke into conversations or smiles or simply hugged each other.

The sense of jubilation was overwhelming. It had been six long years. Almost a year since George had died. And now it was over. Although of course, for many of us the sense of loss hadn't ended.

I shut out any thoughts of what life would be like if George was here. He wasn't and that was that. It didn't stop me from wanting to be happy. He would've wanted that too, I was certain.

'When are we allowed out until to celebrate?' Pat piped up to the matron. To my shock, even the end of the war couldn't raise much of a smile on Matron's stern face.

'It will be ten o'clock,' she said, her lips as tight as ever.

I just couldn't believe it. Only half an hour extra even though the war had ended.

'It just goes to show how strict this place is,' I grumbled to Pat.

We soon forgot though, as we ran to get dressed up and go and join the street parties springing up everywhere.

As it was, we all arrived back after midnight, but not before we'd had the best night out ever. We ended up in St Helens town centre, every single person in the whole of Liverpool (it felt like it anyway!) was dancing in the street to music or playing instruments. Some people just stood and cheered until their throats were hoarse.

I found myself being given a bunk up a lamppost. Clinging to the top, I shouted and cheered at the top of my lungs until my throat hurt. The scene of everyone smiling, clapping and dancing below, turning an ordinary street into a jubilant, energetic party, was one I knew I'd never forget.

It was as if we'd been stuck in a pressure cooker for years and had finally been set free.

Of course, the sadness of George was never far from my mind, but I refused to allow myself to think down that road. I just couldn't.

The following day, we all had sore heads, but all lived in hope now that much better times were around the corner. George wasn't here to see it, but I wasn't the only one to have suffered such a loss. I'd hazard a guess almost all of the folk dancing were doing it through some sadness.

Once again the thought of those Clent Hills sprang to my mind. By now I was truly fed up of nursing. My life felt so restrictive. I'd been put in the boarding schools and then was stuck in nursing homes, seeing the same wards and people day in and day out. I wanted a complete change and it seemed the army was my only chance of doing this.

After putting up with Liverpool for a while longer, I decided to leave and ended up doing various general nursing and nannying jobs while I thought of ways to join the army. I went to work as a nanny for a well-heeled lady in Stafford for a while. The father of the house was a shoe-factory owner, the mother just thought she was God's gift and their two little kids were a pair of horrors. I didn't stay long. Then I briefly went to work for another family in Yorkshire. Three years passed all too quickly and, again, the nagging feeling that I wanted the army life returned.

* * *

By now it was 1948. I'd gone to stay with Ken and his wife Phyllis; he'd met her when she was working the switchboard in the Signals Corps. Ken had left the army and they were living in Great Yarmouth now. I'd always kept in close touch with my brothers. We'd heard from Norman recently and he'd had his own dramas to deal with.

After the war Norman came home to find Julie had had a baby after falling pregnant by one of the American soldiers stationed nearby. Although she was still in love with Norman and wanted to be with him, he couldn't ever forgive her. So he left her and became friends with and eventually married another woman, but that relationship didn't work out. It was all such a shame, but what happened was difficult and in those strange times during the war it could happen to anyone.

One evening I talked late into the night with Ken about what I really wanted to do with my life. I felt so close to him. Although I'd been close to Cliff as kids, in comparison, Ken seemed like a mature man of the world now. He became more of a confidant than ever and liked to look after me, as well as tell me what to do. Sometimes when he walked behind me he'd kick my feet and tease me, saying, 'Walk like a lady!' as a joke. But when it came to serious matters, he really cared.

'It's your life and your decision, Win,' he said, 'but you do seem dead set on it, I must say. I think the army life would do you lots of good. You'd love it.'

*　　*　　*

'I think it's just something I have to do,' I agreed. Nursing didn't make me happy, I'd lost George, and Dad couldn't stop me now.

Just before my twenty-second birthday, on 6 August, I woke up and decided that it was the day to take the plunge. I took myself off to the ATS (Auxilliary Territorial Service) recruitment office and signed up there and then. It was all so easy. I was given a general knowledge test and medical and they accepted me straight away.

It was to be just two weeks later I'd be on my way to Guildford to start training for a whole new career. And way of life. I didn't tell Dad. I'd stopped ringing him already and our visits had dwindled to just a couple of times a year. Olive was always there, in my mind stirring things between us. Her presence felt like a dark cloud, and I felt so unwelcome while she was around, so I just detached myself even further. Not only was I to say goodbye to civvy life, but it was time to say goodbye to something really quite precious.

George's letters.

I'd carried them everywhere with me for the past four years. Always carefully putting them on the bottom of my suitcase so I didn't crush them and always putting them away in a drawer or some place safe near my bed. I'd never read them again, it was too painful, but I couldn't bring myself to get rid of them either.

Now I was about to sign my life away to the army I knew they had to go. I would be travelling with few belongings and I couldn't cart them everywhere, around the world. Not anymore.

I sat with them on my bed one last time, touching the paper where he'd touched, tracing his handwriting with my finger. I closed my eyes and allowed myself to think of him again, as if he were sat right next to me.

Well, George, I thought, if you are alive, captured somewhere, you'll come back and we'll pick up where we left off. If you're not then I have to move on and get rid of these letters anyway . . .

As always, a lump formed in my throat. Four long years had passed and I'd heard nothing from his mother either. I was tempted a few times to contact her but decided it'd probably be all too painful for her. It was still very painful for me.

Without allowing myself another thought, I went downstairs and stoked up the fire in the boiler room. Closing my eyes, I gently tossed each letter on it, watching as the pages curled, smoked and disintegrated. Although this action was taking George's words away from me, I knew nothing could change the way I felt inside about him. One thing I did keep was the one photo I had of him. The one in his civvies he'd sent me, the one taken in case he got shot down. I vowed to keep that for ever.

The day before I left, Ken and his wife happened to be away, so I went to bed filled with excitement, but realised I didn't have an alarm clock to wake me up. I had to search the house for one, but barely slept anyway. I knew a new chapter in my life was about to start.

That morning I ate a quick breakfast before catching the early morning train to London.

It was so thrilling. Only Ken and Cliff knew of my plans. Nobody else. I still hadn't bothered telling my dad. I knew he'd be against it and I was tired of arguing with him, plus my relationship with Olive was no better. By now, I'd had enough and was quite happy to cut him out.

I arrived all hot and nervous in Guildford by the afternoon. My knees had almost turned to water as I waited for the NCO (non-commissioned officer) who took my name and then asked me to step onto the army truck, which basically looked like a vehicle to transport cattle. I waited in silence as more trains arrived and more ladies jumped on. Then the truck door was slammed shut and we rattled off, our spines jarring on each bump. We all looked at each other and smiled politely. Nobody knew what to expect next.

Guildford was to be our home for the next eight weeks while we trained to be soldiers. My heart sank as I spotted all the slightly dilapidated wooden huts and khaki-clad women milling around. It just looked so bleak!

I wondered for the first time what I'd let myself in for. But I'd already told myself firmly: 'Whatever happens, Win, you just put up with it.' There was so much more to army life I was looking forward to. I wanted to travel and see the world. I wanted excitement and a life not set in stone. I knew the army could give me all of this, and if it meant suffering a few hardships along the way then so be it. I knew it'd be worthwhile.

Besides, things in civvy street were far from good in the late 1940s. A lot of the country was suffering from the dreadful aftershocks of war. There was a housing shortage. Many streets were half-bombed. There were few jobs and little money around. People were suffering terribly, both psychologically and in their day-to-day lives. Life outside the army was definitely not a happy place. It seemed as grey and empty as some of the craters still in the roads made by the Luftwaffe.

And now I was prepared to 'rough it' for a bit, I was feeling really upbeat. I knew it'd be worth it in the end. The fitness side of things didn't bother me either, as I'd had to be in good shape for being a nurse.

In our new camp there was so much to take in. We had to navigate our way around where everything was; the sleeping quarters, the cookhouse, medical centre, quartermaster's store . . . it was a whole new world.

On arrival we were medically examined, vaccinated, measured, poked and prodded. Then we were given our regimental numbers, something you are never allowed to forget. I'd have it for the rest of my army career.

We were taught what it meant to be 'lined up in a squad'. This involved all quickly jumping into position in a line. Then we had to stand with square shoulders and start to walk 'in step'. Luckily we had Corporals at the front who'd been doing it for years so we could copy them. If anyone dared fall out of step, you were quickly corrected by a barking voice. We had to swing our arms just to our shoulder height as we went, just so, at the right height. It's harder than it looks! Drill, I was to learn, could be very complicated and involved all kinds of different orders.

A Sergeant's squadron was completely under their control and when they asked you to jump you always did it to the height they wanted. There were around 40 in our squad, and we were all being trained for different things, like cooks, clerks, signals, etc. There was so much to take in and we had to do it quickly.

'Line up straight,' barked the Sergeant.

We almost jumped out of our skins, as we all looked around us to make sure we were straight. The command was much easier said than done.

Next we were told to line up again by the quartermaster's room to go and collect our kit.

It was a slow and chaotic process as nobody had their right size and only a few bits were available on the first day.

'But I don't have any . . .' one lady whined in a nasally voice, when the Sergeant caught her.

'If you're missing something, ladies, then just move on. This isn't a department store for an outfit that suits you. You get what you're given!'

I was handed a pair of trousers (a bit too long), shoes, skirt, tights, knickers, vest, bra, battledress top, all in a fetching shade of khaki (although soon this would change to green when the ATS became the WRAC).

Then, still not having changed into our gear, we were given a basic lesson in marching.

'Everywhere you go, wherever you are going on camp, you are to march there and back, there and back,' shouted our NCO.

That meant even if we were going to use the lavatory. There was to be no loitering around or casual strolling on camp. We had to march everywhere.

Again we lined up and were told to set off. Some of the ladies, already, didn't seem to be up to the challenge. A few of them struggled with keeping in step. 'Right, left, right, left, right, left . . .' shouted our Sergeant.

Then suddenly out of nowhere came: 'HALT!' and you'd stop dead, trying desperately not to bump into the person in front of you or trip up the person behind.

I quite enjoyed it really, but it took some time to get into the swing of it!

We were then told in no uncertain terms where we could and couldn't go. For example, the parade ground was out of bounds and if anyone dared be caught walking (and not marching) anywhere they were in big trouble.

Once a girl forgot. She was late for the canteen and tried to half walk and run across the parade ground to catch up.

'Get yourself over here!' boomed a voice. After a dressing-down from the NCO, she was given a toothbrush and made to scrub the parade ground with it, every square foot!

It was all so much to take in. But because it was so intense, we started to learn very fast indeed.

After learning our drill we often had to go for more medicals or down to the gym to start working out. Everything was about keeping our bodies very fit now.

We soon learned the days were to be long and quite hard. The only respite we got was the chance to sit and natter in the canteen. It was here I got the chance to speak to the other women.

'Why did you join up?' I asked a couple of them. And I was quite surprised by the answer.

'To meet a husband!' one or two giggled. They were quite open about it too. After the war there was a bit of a shortage of men and what better place to mix with the lads than join the army?

After our first long day we all fell gratefully into our beds in the barracks, filled with around thirty single beds.

The next morning we were woken by a 'reveille' at 7 a.m., which took the form of a hand bell rung very hard at the door by our NCO. You had just two or three minutes to be up and standing to attention by your bed. The noise really was enough to wake the dead and it wasn't a pleasant way to emerge from your slumber.

Then the NCO came into our barrack room and told us to put on the kit we'd been issued with.

I only had a top and some trousers, so I put on another blouse underneath and made sure my boots were as shiny as possible. Then, like everyone else, I legged it outside to get into line.

As I peered down the line at the other girls though, I almost couldn't believe what I was seeing.

A couple of the ladies were shivering, wearing big army trousers, but on their top half nothing but their bras! Another couple had khaki tops on but no trousers and you could see the goose bumps on their legs . . . and their knickers on plain view!

I swallowed hard trying not to laugh. I couldn't quite believe some of the women had been so silly. Of course, we had to accept orders to the letter now, but a bit of common sense was also needed.

When the NCO came out, I could tell straight away she wasn't going to see the funny side. Her mouth fell open as she inhaled deeply to blast away any doubt as to her feelings.

'You stupid people . . . what the heck do you think you're DOING?' she screamed, her face turning a shade of beetroot. 'Get yourselves back inside at once and put some clothes – any clothes you have – on.'

Cowering and shaking with the cold, the girls ran in, their wobbly bits all on display. It was hilarious, even if I felt a bit mean laughing.

The thing I hated most about our new life at the time was the meals. We'd been issued with a knife, fork, spoon and tin mug, and were told these were ours to clean and keep safe.

Then every single meal time we had to put on khaki overalls and march quickly with our cutlery to the canteen. I absolutely hated the overalls. They felt so uncomfortable and degrading to wear, almost like we were prisoners.

'All that's missing is a ball and chain,' I overheard someone else grumble.

We had to line up so the canteen staff could serve our food. We held the plate up as the food got slopped on and in many cases you didn't even know what the meal was supposed to be! Not just by the texture or consistency, but sometimes even by the taste. Often it was just stew or mashed potato and meat, but indistinguishable from something you might find in a pig's trough. The veg was always over-boiled and the meat was very stringy. It seemed everything was overcooked and over-salted. But once again I told myself not to complain.

Thankfully we could also get some food in the Salvation Army canteen – the Sally Ann – a bit further down the camp. We had to buy the food ourselves in there and in our case it took a lot of our wages. I was earning just £1/10 or so a week but it was enough to treat myself to a cake or two.

The other treat we could afford was fish'n'chips. Oh my goodness, how I lived for the moment we could slip off camp and go and buy ourselves some from the nearby chippie.

But one of the biggest rules outside the camp was not to be seen eating with our hats on. And as we always had to wear our hats, that meant we couldn't be seen eating in uniform. It was a punishable offence if you were caught.

I soon discovered the best chip shop nearby though, and the chips in those days were utterly delicious. They were fluffy on the inside and cooked to perfection in lard. Sometimes, when I managed to buy some, all wrapped up in newspaper, I'd slip out of the shop, look both ways for any loitering NCO, and find the nearest alleyway.

Then I'd lean against the brick wall, close my eyes and relish the taste, as if it were a little piece of heaven on earth. Never ever had fish'n'chips tasted so good!

Although I was used to living with groups of people from my days at the convent and in nursing, I also learned army life and the hierarchy system that came with it meant you couldn't always trust everyone.

In the first week I took my clothes off to go to gym, and saw I still had the gold watch on my mother had given me all those years ago. I took it off and wondered what to do with it to keep it safe. A Corporal was standing watch so I gave it to her.

'Would you mind looking after this for me if possible?' I asked politely. She nodded in agreement and dropped it in her pocket.

At the end of the session, I went to approach the Corporal to ask for it back but she looked right through me.

'Right, everyone, time to move on to drill,' she barked, turning her back on me.

A feeling of horror washed through me as I realised there and then I wasn't going to get it back. You weren't supposed to approach the Corporals for anything, it was tantamount to an offence to do so, and I suppose I shouldn't even have asked for my watch to be minded.

Now she'd stolen it, that much I could sense.

After that I always watched my belongings like a hawk and never asked anyone to look after anything, especially a mean superior who could abuse their position.

Early on we had interviews to find out about what jobs we'd like to take up within the army.

I had my heart set on being a switchboard operator, I'm not sure why. Maybe it was because Ken had been in signals and met his wife doing this job. It sounded interesting, taking calls from all over the world. I knew it would keep me on my toes and never be dull at least.

I sat down and, after I'd politely answered a few questions, my interviewer rustled some papers and looked up.

'You're going to be a teleprinter operator,' she said primly. 'Your training will begin next . . .'

But before she could continue I found myself interrupting her.

'Actually, I'd like to be a switchboard operator,' I said.

She looked up and stared at me in shock.

'Well, *actually* . . . you're going to be a teleprinter operator and you will do as you're told,' she said.

Somehow, the way she spoke to me once again triggered the little girl inside, the one who hated being told what to do and would fight for her voice to be heard. My voice came out loudly and measured.

'If you put me down as a teleprinter operator,' I said slowly, 'I will simply leave at the end of this week. I would like to be a switchboard operator. Please.'

She opened her mouth as if to argue, but then scribbled something down instead.

'Yes, yes, OK, you will be trained in switchboard operations,' she conceded.

I saluted her and marched smartly out, thinking I was so glad I'd spoken up.

Somehow, I managed to survive those first few weeks, and I dare say even enjoyed it.

We'd been taught how to wear our uniform properly, how to march, what drill was, and how to salute. Of course, we also had to keep our bedding in immaculate order, just like everything else. So as soon as we woke we were up, folding and smoothing the sheets and blankets, so the edges were as straight as a rule. All beds had to be stripped, the bedding folded and wrapped around the pillow in a strictly neat and tidy manner and placed perfectly at the end of the bare mattress. My nursing training came in very useful.

One thing we hadn't been shown anything of though was weaponry. I knew this was to be the case in the ATS, as no woman ever worked at the front line and nobody was taught anything about ammunitions or weapons. And this was the way I liked it. If I had been asked to shoot or use a gun I'd never have countenanced joining up. To me, being in the army didn't have to mean killing or injuring anyone.

A few of the squad were lost along the way, as they weren't seen as suitable for army life, normally having problems with fitness or attitude. We never got to say goodbye either. They simply disappeared one afternoon and never came back.

But most of us had made it and we had a small passing-out parade. I felt very pleased with myself.

Chapter Eight

In the Army Now

The next stop was our signals training camp in Catterick. It was a very big, sprawling place and of course, we still had to march everywhere and wear those terrible khaki overalls as we went to our meals. I ended up having to get an extra pair of shoes as I quickly worn down the soles, marching so much.

The meals were something else altogether. If we'd thought the food was bad in Guildford, nothing could have prepared us for this. And the canteen staff this time seemed to take great delight in this. The way they violently slopped the food at us meant if our plates were not directly underneath at the moment they robotically served the 'food' it dropped unceremoniously at our feet (not unlike something you'd find on a pavement after an untrained dog had been around).

It turned my stomach just to see it, let alone think about eating it! Sometimes I felt like a lucky one if my portion missed the bowl.

I started losing weight as I hated the food so much. Luckily there were a few other canteens again, just like the Sally

Ann's, provided by the churches, so we just ate in there, but I still dropped down to eight stone or so.

These little havens were like life-savers to us as not only could we get something half-decent to eat, we could also sit and chat. I soon realised how friendly most people were in the army. It was a case of 'everyone was in it together'.

It was there I met Betty. She was a lovely lass. Her boyfriend was in the submarines and she always talked about him proudly. It was a scary, horrible-sounding job and one I could never do . . . living miles under the sea? No, thank you.

I was very happy to be meeting new people and making new friends though. We were from all walks of life, all parts of the country, but we all wanted the same thing. To enjoy ourselves as much as possible and give this new way of life our all.

Sometimes we even managed to escape the camp for the evening and go to the local pub with the lads who were training on the other side of the camp. One evening, I was with my friend Betty when we took a wrong turn down a road on the way back.

'Are you sure this is the right way?' I asked, nervously. The roads looked dark and I couldn't recognise any of the signs.

'It must be,' said Betty.

But as the road widened out and more unrecognisable landmarks came into view, I started to have doubts.

'Oh goodness, look at the time,' I cried as we passed a church clock.

It was ten to ten and we had just ten minutes to get back. We both turned and started running back up the lane.

'We're going to be for it when we get back,' I cried.

Betty started panicking now too. 'Sorry!' she said. 'It's all my fault.'

Thank goodness we found the right crossroads and ran as fast as we could to 'book' back in the camp. But of course an officer was already there, grim-faced.

Tapping her watch, she marched us straight to the commanding officer. He looked down his nose at us and told us to go and report to our NCO the following day.

After a bad night's sleep worrying what would happen, we were handed our sentence: two hours' extra duties for two evenings.

The following night we reported to our Orderly Sergeant after our evening meal – on went the dreaded khaki overalls, and we were handed a bucket, scrubbing brush and broom. Then, as the other squads jeered and laughed at us, we were made to march to the offices on the other side of the camp and start cleaning them from top to bottom. It was so boring and made my back ache and my hands shrivel and hurt.

'Urgh,' I muttered to Betty as we finished. 'This really is the pits!'

By now it was November and the weather turned very harsh suddenly. The barrack rooms were extremely cold and my chilblains flared up again. My skin became red raw and swollen all over my hands, feet and legs. The army doctor looked at it but there was little they could do. The barracks were cold and our stove in the room wasn't enough to heat it up. They weren't going to suddenly get a paraffin heater just for one recruit, so I just had to put up with it. It affected me so badly that operating the switchboard became almost impossible. You needed quick and nimble fingers to get it right and I just couldn't.

Although I picked up on how to operate the board quickly and I passed my theory exams with flying colours, my chilblains held me back with the practical exams. So I was 'back-squadded', which meant another two weeks in Yorkshire, retaking exams.

Finally, as my skin calmed down and I could press buttons properly again, I passed!

It had taken four months, stomaching some dreadful food and intense cold but I'd done it. I was a trained soldier. I was Private Phillips. Now I would always be known as Phillips or 'Phill' for short, never Win or Winifred. My next posting would be as a fully fledged switchboard operator and I'd be stationed in Aldershot.

Aldershot was enormous, with thousands of troops living in the garrison town, but it was also a normal town, with ordinary civvies in it. This made me feel like it was a more 'human' place to be in a way. But if I'd hoped our camp in Aldershot would be any more pleasant than what I'd seen so far I was disappointed.

Our living quarters were bad. They'd been built many years before 1948, and didn't look like they'd seen a lick of paint since. And they were very cold. We had one black stove burning coke in the middle, but were only allowed to stoke it up at 5 p.m. and only for two hours. And this particular winter was bitter.

Coke doesn't last long either, but some ingenious person realised where the coke store was, so some of the brave girls slipped off and jumped over the wall.

I watched with baited breath, hoping our NCO wouldn't suddenly turn up.

'Quick,' I hissed, as I heard their feet crunching on bits of coke.

Suddenly a few big pieces were tossed over the wall, landing at my feet.

'Give us a hand,' whispered one of the girls, as she appeared on the wall. We held hands as she jumped down. Then we grabbed the pieces and flitted back to the quarters before anyone noticed.

A few nights we were able to enjoy a toasty evening thanks to them.

Of course, romances often blossomed between some of the girls and lads. Relationships were not banned, even if they did distract attentions sometimes! They probably couldn't have been stopped if our superiors had tried. There were plenty of quiet places for a bit of a cuddle, with lots of fields and woods nearby.

I wasn't interested at this time though, even if I'd met anyone lovely. I suppose, somewhere deep inside, I'd made a decision not to fall for anyone again. Not like George. I'd been hurt so badly, I never ever wanted to have to live through that again.

The men were always around during drinks breaks, or sometimes in the canteen, and occasionally they'd stagger back from the pub after a few drinks and find themselves in our quarters . . . all by accident.

Our block was in between two male blocks, one of them occupied by paratroopers. It was a mistake easily made in the dark. All three barracks looked identical. We'd hear them staggering in, singing softly, and everyone would yell in unison: 'Wrong place!' before dissolving into laughter as we heard them stumble off.

As usual, everything around our beds had to be in apple pie order and we had to 'barrack' our beds. It was a real effort at first but we all became dab hands in the end. It did take a few minutes though, and we'd always offer to do our neighbour's sheets if they were on a late shift.

There was no hot water in our barrack block, so the only chance of a good hot bath was down the road at the bathhouse. What a joy it was to sink beneath some steam and feel your limbs loosen! The only down side was walking back to the barracks afterwards . . . you'd soon feel like an ice-cube again. We also had to always be in full uniform, even just to leave the barracks for a bath. It was tedious getting dressed and re-dressed, but we weren't allowed to be mistaken for civvies.

My new job on the switchboard was tough. It was very tiring concentrating on the boards all day, plugging in and taking out. But, like I imagined it would be, it was an interesting job. I got to speak to operators from all over and you had to keep on your toes all day, so time whizzed past.

There were around fifteen of us operating the telephone system for the whole of Aldershot and you had to concentrate to connect people properly. We were known as Aldershot 380. We mainly answered the phone to army personnel, but sometimes we put through calls from the public too, depending on what they wanted.

After a few weeks, I felt comfortable in my job. It was incredibly hard work though, and we weren't even allowed a break for a cup of tea. You had to concentrate hard for hours on end and were obliged to keep incredibly calm under pressure, always answering the phone very politely, even under duress or with rude callers. We simply didn't dare do anything otherwise!

One day, however, a rude officer made a remark to one of the girls. In his view his call hadn't been picked up fast enough.

'You're just a lazy lot!' he cried. 'What are you up to in there? Nattering away or something, eh?'

The girl grew incensed. It was very hard constant work on the switchboard. You didn't have a minute to think, let alone natter. Even if you needed to spend a penny you had to raise your hand and wait patiently until someone could cover you. We were all highly diligent, taking our roles in keeping the phone lines open very seriously. This disrespectful officer really put this girl's nose out of joint.

She slammed down her headset. She was sorely fed up now. With no break, we all felt pretty much the same way.

'Right,' she said, after recounting his comments. 'Let's show him! Strike!'

She started chanting 'strike, strike' and soon a frisson of rebellion swept across the room and we were all throwing down our headsets. We folded our arms and sat in silence as we watched the boards light up like fireworks, going crazy.

Our supervisor came rushing out.

'What's going on?' she cried.

'We're fed up,' said one girl.

'We're not lazy but get told we are,' said another.

'And we're not even allowed a break,' I chimed in.

'Well, you can't just sit there,' the supervisor began. 'Get back on the phones.'

But she could tell by our faces we'd reached breaking point and she ran off to find an officer to help. Our mini-strike went on for several hours before the top brass worked out what to do. We were to get breaks, for one thing, although an apology from that rude officer would've been nice too!

While I was in Aldershot, the NAAFI club was opened by HRH Duke of Gloucester and we all immediately loved the place.

The NAAFI, short for the Navy, Army and Air Force Institutes, was set up in 1921 to run fun and necessary establishments for the armed forces; this included everything from cafés to launderettes to bars for the soldiers to use or relax in. It was a real blessing in what was quite a bleak living area. We spent many of our off-duty hours dancing, eating, relaxing and having a laugh there. It was a welcome (and warm!) break from our living quarters and our commissioned officers weren't allowed in, so we could really take our hats off and let our hair down.

I'd only been in the army for six months when in March 1949 the chance of a posting abroad working on switchboards came up. We all knew the chances of being posted abroad were high, but you never knew when it would be or where, it all depended on what you were trained in and what they needed.

When the news came in that I'd be headed to Port Said in Egypt I was completely thrilled.

'I've done it!' I cried to Betty. 'I'm going to see the world now!'

It would be the first time ever I'd be going abroad. Betty was equally pleased though. Her boyfriend had proposed and she was leaving to get married. I knew I'd miss her, but at the same time being tied down was the last thing I wanted!

Finally we were given the dates and times for our boat and then given a few weeks' leave. This would be our chance to say goodbye to everyone before we disappeared from these shores for two years.

I got train tickets to go and stay with Ken again, and I was looking forward to seeing him.

But as I packed up my belongings, Betty came rushing in.

'Phill,' she said, breathlessly, 'you've got to report to the office as the draft has been postponed.'

I laughed.

'Yes, Betty,' I said, carrying on folding my clothes. 'Pull the other one.'

'No, really!' she cried. 'I promise you it's no joke . . . it's all on hold.'

The look on her face persuaded me she was being honest, so I dropped everything and rushed to the office.

'You have to make your bedding up again now,' said the NCO. 'Your draft has been delayed by two weeks.'

My heart started banging and I started to feel very anxious. Stupidly, it never occurred to me the army had good reasons for delaying things, and my imagination ran away with me. I wondered if it was because something was going to happen to the ship and this was fate telling me I shouldn't go! Or perhaps they'd even change their minds at the end of the two weeks and I'd never get to go abroad. Maybe I'd be stuck in Aldershot.

But a few weeks later, I went through the ritual of handing in my bedding and collecting railway warrants. Then, without waiting to have another cup of tea in the canteen, I went straight to the station. We had to go to Brighton to our holding bay and drafting unit to wait for the big 'off'.

We were set to spend ten days on a boat travelling there, no easy task with floating mines left over from the war still a huge problem in the Mediterranean and some areas. But even that didn't faze me now. This was my big chance and a few mines weren't going to put me off.

Waiting for our posting to come up was very boring though as we were moved to a barracks in Brighton to wait for the big day. All we had to do were mundane jobs, like polishing corridors (and there seemed to be miles of them), peeling potatoes and washing pots and pans or scrubbing toilets, so we spent more time trying to think of fun ways to entertain ourselves. None of us were even allowed out of the camp though, and we didn't have any money even if we could escape for a couple of hours.

However, someone discovered a busy chip shop across the road at the edge of the camp. It was decided one day we could try and go over in twos, sneaking across the road and meeting up there.

In pairs, we sauntered to the edge of the camp, then when no one was looking we nipped over to the chippie. Staggering our escape, we eventually all ended up there.

The shop owner couldn't have known what hit him as suddenly his tables were filled with chattering khaki-clad ladies, all very pleased with themselves and their temporary escape.

We ordered portions of chips and they tasted like little pieces of fried heaven after the slop we'd been served over the last few weeks. The windows were fairly steamed up with all the extra frying, so we felt quite safe we wouldn't be spotted by any passing NCO.

After a good half an hour, someone arrived at the door, breathless.

'The RSM wants you all back now!' she said.

Suddenly the chip I was eating felt stuck in my throat. 'Oh, blimey!' I cried. 'We're for it now!'

We all left what we were eating and said goodbye to the owner before setting off to face the music. And it wasn't a pretty sight. The RSM's face was shaking with rage.

'What do you think you're all doing?' she bellowed. 'If this EVER happens again you will lose your posting abroad and never ever be sent overseas again.'

I inwardly gasped. This would've been a nightmare. Although afterwards, I did wonder whether they'd really go that far with a punishment.

The following day we set off for Liverpool, where our boat was sailing from. Just beforehand we were issued with our new kit. It included a deep sea bag, with a blanket.

'What's this for?' somebody asked.

'This,' explained our NCO, 'is a blanket into which you will be sewn if anything should happen at sea and you die, and in which you will then be tossed overboard. It's known as the "death blanket".'

We all smiled uneasily at each other. A shiver of excitement rushed through me.

Chapter Nine

True Escape

As we waited while our boat was prepared, my good friend from the hospital in Prescot, Pat, came to see me off. It meant so much to me, just spending some time together over coffee. Just having a friendly face to say goodbye to was wonderful.

'I can't believe how far away you'll be,' said Pat as we warmed our hands around our coffee. 'You really are terribly brave.'

I laughed. 'It's the only thing that will make me happy, Pat,' I said. 'Ever since I first saw maps of the world, I've wanted to get away. Two years might sound like a long time to be away but it'll fly by.'

She gave me a big hug as I got up to leave.

'Rather you than me, Win,' she said. 'But one thing's for sure. You're not missing much at the hospital.'

And I knew she was right.

Climbing aboard that boat was terribly exciting. Perhaps due to my upbringing I very much had the notion life should be grabbed with both hands with no hesitation. And finally I felt alive.

All our excitement was dampened slightly when we were ordered to wear full uniform at all times and carry on with extra duties of washing and ironing as if we were back in barracks!

But aside from this, we were treated very well. In fact, the women were allowed to stay above deck and dine in the same room as the officers. The food was amazing; after our canteen stuff, it tasted so good and we put enough of it away. We were also told the ATS was changing its name to the WRAC (Women's Royal Army Corps), but it all felt a bit strange to me and certainly didn't trip off my tongue.

Our first stop was Malta. As we glided into the harbour, we were all agog at the pretty picture-postcard white buildings and the sand which got everywhere. The sun was shining and it all seemed very exotic.

The first thing that hit me was the noise. The boat was surrounded by locals and soldiers, all speaking loudly, incomprehensibly in foreign languages. It sounded to me like parrots squawking.

Many of the market traders were trying to sell us something or other and throwing baskets on strings on board.

'What are they doing?' I gasped, leaning further over the rail.

'Who knows?' said one of the women. 'But it looks like they're making the officers haggle for it whatever it is.'

We Privates didn't have any money so could only watch in awe as the baskets filled with tobacco or chocolate or other bits and pieces came flying up and down to loud cries. Neither were we allowed off ship for the evening, so we had to wave off the officers who all marched off to look around the shops or get a meal in a café. Afterwards they kindly brought us back some sweets and chocolate. Not all of them were bad at all. Of course there was still rationing in place, even on our boat, so the sight of these colourful sweet wrappers and other delights was very welcome.

Then we weighed anchor again and off we set towards our final destination of Port Said.

This time a Z craft, a low boat usually used for carrying luggage, came to collect us off the ship. Pulling into Egypt was another incredible sight. For me it felt a little like I was in a film.

Mauritian police were marching up and down on shore to protect us. We weren't welcome in Egypt after the war. We were seen as outsiders and not a peaceful influence, even though the whole point of us being there was to have a benign presence.

As we marched onto dry land, I soon got a real taste of how the tensions were only simmering underneath the sunshine when a young Arab jumped on a policeman and tried to stab him with a knife as we marched past. He was wrestled to the ground within a few seconds but it was enough to leave me shaking a little. We weren't allowed to show it though and had to keep our shoulders back, head up and eyes to the front.

'Keep marching,' barked our NCO.

It reminded me of the dangers we were facing.

The strong smell of kerosene hit me as we walked to our trucks for the next part of our journey. All the cafés and outdoor markets seemed to use this heating source and it almost burned the hairs in my nostril. Even now, when I smell kerosene I immediately think: Egypt!

We were driven to the train station and with a little more chaos and lots of Arab men shouting at us, we were bustled onto the carriages.

The chaos of the outside didn't disappear once we pulled away from the station. The roof of the train was teeming with local men hitching a ride, but now all peering and leering into our windows. The presence of white female members of the army was not going unnoticed.

We all found it quite funny, but our RSM didn't. She rushed up and down the carriages pulling down the blinds to spoil the men's view and our fun. It became even more of a farce though, as the blinds needed fastening at the bottom and as fast as she pulled them down they pinged straight back up again!

Nobody was really helping her keep them down as we all found it so amusing. Some of the men grew more excited as they started pulling down their trousers to wave their dangly bits at us. We were almost rolling around in the aisles, weeping with laughter.

One of them, Pauline, managed to get a window open a little.

'You want my sex stimulant,' he leered, then yelped as someone snapped the window shut on his fingers.

'Wish we'd caught the private parts,' Pauline said, as we all dissolved into more giggles.

It was a real eye-opener for many of us though. Goodness, I thought, as things finally settled down and the blinds were finally closed. If this is life in the real Egypt what are we letting ourselves in for?

Finally we arrived at Ismalia. The heat was intense and baking hot, but we had our uniforms of short sleeves and sandals to tailor to it.

Some of the women found the conditions too much to bear and complained of prickly heat and feeling tired or sick. I loved it though. After spending so long shivering over coke stoves or suffering from chilblains this was heaven for me and I was determined not to complain!

This time we didn't have to queue for our food. We were waited on by Sudanese waiters, who looked most peculiar to us wearing their white djellabas and red fezzes.

'Maybe the food will taste fit for a king, if we're being treated to waiters bringing it to us,' I joked.

But even though the food was brought to us, it was still almost inedible. Even worse, the cooks tried to mimic English food of meat and two veg, but a lot of it was nondescript sludge, with the added bonus of a good sprinkling of gritty sand all over it.

I soon started to lose weight again, as I turned down a lot of the platefuls. But apart from that, I was very happy to be out of Blighty, at least for a couple of years.

Ismalia, I discovered, was one of the most fertile spots in Egypt and had a huge French population, so was quite a sophisticated place with parks and gardens everywhere and a canal called the Sweet Water Canal flowing through it. Its name was a bit misleading as it was one of the filthiest waterways I'd ever seen and it stunk to high heaven. People were always washing in it or using it as a loo and I lost count of the number of cows, sheep or unidentified dead animals spotted floating on the surface of it.

We didn't need to be told twice to keep away from it. There were so many diseases rife, but one especially nasty one was bilharzia – a bug that burrowed under your skin and could attack every part of your body. It sounded like something from outer space to me, and I was always very careful about drinking water and avoiding risks.

We also soon discovered how often the locals went to pray, with the unmistakable sound of the mosque call to prayer every day, starting at 4 a.m. It was greeted by us with groans and pillows held over our heads.

I was among those posted to Fayid, so that was my next stop, a bit further up the canal.

Our camp had been a hospital during the war and was a big brick building. We were shown our places to eat and sleep and it was all very basic, but I was used to this by now. I was in a barracks with nineteen other women and it was very hot with little furniture, but I didn't miss the cold or the coke burner in the middle!

We were all given mosquito nets but the ordeal involved in putting it up meant I didn't bother with it. Sadly though, the mozzies still bothered with me, and I ended up half-eaten alive by the end of the first night.

We had large fans on the ceiling but they made a huge

racket once they got going and caused quite an icy draught to whoever was in the wrong spot, so we all argued over whether they should go on or stay off.

We had no hot water and only buckets for a loo. The hot water was easy to warm up on our paraffin stove though, and of course when it was so hot outside we were quite happy to have cool water to wash ourselves in.

Going to the loo was more of a chore on those buckets. They were emptied by the locals, who certainly didn't seem to have any qualms about this particularly unpleasant job. They'd empty them every morning via a door in the wall and were very quick in doing this. Sometimes they'd even pull the bucket from under whoever was spending a penny. A few of the girls complained about this!

Our new home appeared to be a series of buildings dumped in a desert but wasn't horrible at all. Right outside the gates there was also a shopping centre with a NAAFI shop and milk bar, and then a few native shops where you could get souvenirs. There was also an eating house and a hotel and roller-skating rink.

Then about a mile away was Fayid village. The shops there were very basic – just shacks with corrugated-iron roofs on top.

On our first trip into the village we laughed our heads off at the signs.

'Look at this one,' screamed Pauline. 'It says Woolworths.'

We also spotted a 'Harrods', 'Jock McGregor's' and other well-known names of the time. The shops were also people's houses and homes for their pets too, filled with donkeys, goats, hens and goats . . . it was like a zoo. The market was a constant cacophony of chickens and dogs and people shouting.

We soon learned some of the tricks of the area though. In the nearby market, where they sold everything from food to saris, the market traders appeared to love Scottish people and their accents. So I used to try and put one on if I was asking for something, as they'd always find it to sell then! I was fascinated by the way the Egyptians lived. They were always rather cheerful, even though they seemed so poor.

We were lucky enough to have the NAAFI nearby, on the shore of the lake called Bitter Lake. Each rank had its own club, this included Warrant Officers and Sergeants, other ranks, officers and women. I loved the women's club. There was a large expanse of beach where we could sunbathe and swim.

'You coming in, Pauline?' I asked on our first visit.

We all ran into the warm, blue waters, splashing each other and diving below. But Pauline soon came up screaming.

'Oh my giddy aunt, look at what's down there!' she cried.

I looked down at my feet and realised the waters were teeming with colourful fish of every description. I'd never swum so fast, as I could feel them whipping around my toes and knees.

'Urgh!' I cried. 'Get me out of here!'

* * *

The weather was something else to get used to in Egypt, not only the heat but also the whirlwinds. All of a sudden, gusts of air would swirl up and you'd see the wind moving across the trees or the beach, picking up everything in its path. They always gave me the creeps. I was never caught in one, but I hated the thought of being swept up. At the very least it would ruin my hair. And of course, it meant more sand was sent everywhere too.

There were also some amazing sights with the water spouts in the lake. I don't know what caused them but suddenly water would jump like a fountain up in the middle and we'd all be amazed at the display. I just loved the fact everything was so different from anything I'd seen before.

Being a woman in Egypt wasn't easy though. We weren't allowed out at night without a male escort. This seems crazy now, but actually it was a sensible precaution. Not only did your male friend have to meet you at the gate, but they had to sign for you in a book in the guard's hut, stating in writing where you were going.

This was so tedious, and if you didn't get back on time – our curfew was midnight – then they'd alert the military police and a massive full-scale search went on. They didn't want to take any chances and of course it made you sure you'd be punctual on your return.

I'd already learned my lesson from being late back in my training camp anyway, and had finally become a very good timekeeper.

On Monday nights we weren't allowed out at all. In fact, it was the worst night of the week. First of all we had to stay in camp, then the quartermaster's store was opened and if anyone needed any new kit items or whatever they could get it. Then it was time for kit checks; this meant we had to clean everything so it was spotless and have it closely inspected by our superiors.

Often we'd find items were missing however hard we tried. It was always a sock or a pair of knickers or something small. Then we'd have to troop off to the QM store to replace it.

Then it was lights out by 9.30 p.m. – this was to make sure we had at least one early night . . . even if we didn't want one!

We soon discovered that it wasn't always our fault if pieces of our kit went walkabout. The Arab cleaners were not to be entirely trusted. Although they kept the camp spotless, they also seemed to particularly enjoy 'cleaning up' our washing line. Our smalls kept disappearing on a daily basis and nobody knew where to!

It got to the point where some of us ladies were growing quite short on pants and bras, and these were not easily replaced.

One day, I was about to go on midday shift when I spotted a line of cleaners near the quartermaster's store, all in front of a rather irate Sergeant. I watched with interest.

'Get yourselves straight and then do as I say,' he barked at them.

They tried to straighten up, all looking smart as usual in their djellabas.

'Now take your djellabas OFF!' he yelled.

I stifled a giggle. What on earth was he telling them that for?

They seemed to look at each other and then slowly peeled off their layers, to reveal their semi-naked bodies . . . complete with our bras, pants and slips, wound around their midriffs or various limbs. It was the most amusing sight!

There they stood, looking absolutely ridiculous, not knowing quite what to do.

I quickly walked off before anyone spotted me watching, but later on, the Sergeant involved told us proudly he had located our missing garments, and we could come and collect them. But after seeing what I had, I decided he could keep any of mine, thank you very much!

We soon settled in. Although life had changed for all of us, there were still familiar things from home cropping up. The Egyptians love fast motorbike racing, and one day someone mentioned Billie Bates would be racing at an event. Now I loved going with my brother to the speedway track to watch the riders when I stayed in Great Yarmouth, and Billie Bates was a big name. So this was brilliant.

But although I couldn't wait to book tickets we had little money and couldn't afford them. So I managed to put in a call to the place so I could sell programmes and get in for free. I asked the other girls if they wanted to join me.

'Yes, please,' said one I'd bonded with in particular, Alice.

So I made the arrangements, without really thinking

about the next step . . . how we'd actually travel there! We couldn't get public transport on our own.

Even going out after dark was difficult and we had to go everywhere in twos. Making our own way to a speedway show was going to be tricky. Then another officer mentioned a possible way. 'Try and ask Captain Richards, he often organises transport up to the racing, he loves it,' he suggested.

And so I found myself calling Bertie Richards, not knowing I was about to meet someone quite special.

I'd not been interested in anyone after George, and love affairs of any kind didn't attract me. But with Bertie it was different. He was a tall, handsome man, with a lovely way about him.

'Yes, Phill,' he said, when I explained our situation. 'I'll be happy to drive you and the girls.'

It felt a bit cheeky asking a captain, but at the same time he seemed amenable to helping.

I soon heard other stories about this particular captain. Alice told me she'd heard he'd been captured in the war, but had managed to escape.

'Well, he's a brave fellow then, like my brother,' I said. I didn't expect to ask him about it though. It was the unwritten rule about the war, you didn't speak about it. So many terrible, terrible things had happened, people were only able to cope if they put it behind them and tried to think positively and not bring it up. I'd learned that in my own life with George, and also with Norman. He was my brother but not once did he tell us what happened while he was a POW.

On the day of the races, Bertie happily drove us there and back, and I found him to be very chatty, despite the fact I was a much lower rank than him. He was horse mad and was always at the races of the cars or animals. He often refereed the boxing matches between the troops too. All in all he was a bit of an action man and thrill seeker. And to me, he made good, fun company.

When we got back to the barracks he asked for a word with me.

'I'd like to take you out,' he said. 'What do you think to that?'

I was speechless. He was a lovely man, but I was just a Private, and he was a captain. I didn't know for sure, but I could guess this wasn't the done thing.

As I hesitated, I could see he was hanging on for my reply.

'Yes, why not!' I said cheerfully. 'That would be very nice, Bertie.'

His face relaxed and he gave me a wink. 'I'll look forward to it,' he said.

I walked away, wondering what the other girls would think, but then pushed the worry from my mind. It was nobody's business but mine and if whatever happened was low-key then what was the worst that could happen?

Chapter Ten

Under the Sun

Bertie and I quickly grew close, and saw each other most evenings. Although I liked him very much though, I didn't see him as a serious boyfriend. To me, George had been 'The One'. I didn't expect anyone else, including this captain, to match up.

We did all kinds of fun things together but I tended to keep out of his way around the other girls back at the barracks. If someone was marching along and whispered, 'Hey, Bertie is back there,' I'd promptly turn heel and go in the other direction. I didn't think any good could come of us being 'seen'.

We had our ways of keeping in contact though. Often Bertie would ring the switchboard when I was on shift to arrange our next night out. But speaking privately was banned. The system was for the army not our social lives – that was made very clear!

But Bertie, being quite sneaky, used to ring and I'd see his number, 710, flash up. I'd always quickly answer it and because he knew there was a risk my supervisor would be listening in and we'd get into trouble, he'd 'pretend' to talk to someone else.

'George,' he'd command, as if talking to someone from across his room. 'I'll see you at 7 p.m. outside the bar, and bring the cards . . . OK, sorry, operator, could you put me through to extension 120 [the barracks] please.' Clever Bertie!

Then I knew where and when to meet him that night. It used to crack me up, although of course I always kept an efficient straight face.

Our little 'system' of keeping in touch and arranging our social life worked very well until one day his call went astray and someone else picked it up, and somehow they guessed what was going on.

I was hauled up by the officer in charge of the exchange. 'We heard you making a personal call,' she said, angrily.

I tried to pull my best 'puzzled' expression, then tried to insist it wasn't me.

'It was you, Private Phillips,' she replied carefully. It was a tone of voice I knew to back down from.

I nodded. 'Yes, ma'am.' I knew she was on to me and telling fibs now would get me nowhere.

'It must never happen again,' she snapped, before dismissing me. I wondered afterwards if Bertie would also be in trouble. As a captain though, he probably wouldn't be.

I did enjoy spending time with Bertie, not least because he'd take me for the most wonderful meals at nearby restaurants and hotels.

'You need feeding up, Win,' he'd say. 'You'll waste away if you don't eat.'

And it was true. I was so skinny, as I could barely stomach the sand-infused food we were presented with in camp.

We always had a good chat over dinner, talking about camp life or what races he'd seen recently. He taught me a few words of Egyptian too. Within a few weeks I'd learned to ask for 'a cup of tea without sugar but plenty of milk, please'.

Bertie was very fond of me, but I sensed it would only ever be a romance to last the time we were in Egypt; we never spoke of our future. He admired me for my independence and sense of fun. Long term, neither of us thought of settling down. He was protective of me though. There were dodgy things happening all the time in Egypt, like small fights or muggings, or pickpocketing, sometimes in the unlikeliest of places.

One evening I was sitting with Bertie outside the club. The low sunset made the sky a beautiful red and it was so relaxing to just be sitting by the sea, hearing the waves lap on the shore.

Before our next drinks arrived, I decided to spend a penny.

'Just popping down to the ladies,' I said. I walked across the sand, marvelling at the sky and thinking of what we were going to have for dinner. Just as I approached the ladies' block, I saw a girl walking very fast out of the loo. Her friend was waiting outside.

'Do you fancy some?' I overheard her friend ask her, offering some chocolate she was eating.

'No!' she cried, shaking her head, marching away quickly. She looked as if she'd seen a ghost.

I wondered what was wrong with her, but didn't think anything more as I entered the lavatory.

I closed the door behind me and started to pull down my clothing, when suddenly, I felt a hand grabbing at my private parts. It was so frightening, I almost fell over, but scrambled to my feet, pulling on my underwear, and fell out of the door, gripped with panic. I instantly guessed it was some locals trying to assault us and my heart was banging like crazy as I ran quickly back across the beach.

I felt so embarrassed, ashamed. How dare someone try a trick like that!

'Can we go back to the barracks?' I gasped at Bertie.

He looked startled, putting down his drink. 'Phill, whatever has happened?' he said.

'Nothing,' I spluttered, unable to look him in the eye. My cheeks were burning with indignation. 'I just want to go back. Now, please.'

'Tell me,' Bertie persisted, grabbing my shoulders.

I pointed to the block. 'A hand reached out and grabbed me,' I spluttered. Before I'd even finished the sentence, Bertie was running like a crazy hare across the sand.

I went back to the room and tried to put the visions of the fat hairy hand out of my mind. It was so very unsettling and shaming.

Several minutes later Bertie returned. 'I found the barbed wire around the ladies cut into pieces. They'd removed the bucket so they could fit their hand in the hole. I didn't catch any of them at it though.'

I nodded. I just wanted to put the whole sordid business behind me and went back to camp and to bed early.

The following morning the RSM wanted to see me. 'I

heard there was an incident last night. Can you tell me why didn't you report it?' she snapped.

'I didn't want to talk about it then,' I explained.

'Well, you should've reported it all the same,' she insisted. 'Now tell me what happened.'

As I recounted the previous night's events, she started smirking. Then she grabbed her handkerchief, shaking her shoulders as she stifled her laughs. But I just continued, straight-faced, looking forward to getting out of her office. I was sure she wouldn't find it so amusing if it'd happened to her.

Afterwards, word got round about the hand in the loo story and all the girls taunted me. 'Who's dat down d'ere!' they shouted when they saw me.

Eventually I too saw the funny side. Again, it was the only way to deal with the situation.

I was embarrassed for a time. Soon afterwards Bertie arranged for us to go for dinner with another officer and his wife, but I wasn't so sure.

'What if they've heard about the "Dat down d'ere" incident?' I asked.

'So what?' said Bertie. 'I'm sure no one will say anything.'

I went along but could sense they did know and nobody wanted to talk about it. So as usual I put on a brave face.

Halfway through my stint in Egypt they sent half of our regiment to Kenya. There was trouble brewing there but I really didn't want to go. I wanted to stay put, I was having a ball and of course Bertie was there. Luckily they didn't put my name down.

Bertie and I were a good match, in part because we were both so independent. We never talked about our pasts, never spoke about our families or exes or anything. We just got on well and had a nice time together. I liked his company, he liked mine and that was that.

Sometimes I went to extreme lengths not to be seen with Bertie or to avoid people watching me. One day it looked like I'd come unstuck. Bertie was due to give a talk to the regiment about his time escaping from the prisoner of war camp. I was surprised he was doing such a talk as he'd never spoken about the experience to me. But I wasn't keen on everyone in the audience eyeballing me for my reaction or to see if we ever looked at each other.

When it came to the big evening, everyone got ready after dinner to go and hear it. I hung back in the quarters.

'You know you'll have to go,' said Alice, who knew of my reluctance. 'The NCO will be checking our rooms to make sure.'

'Yes,' I sighed.

But I had other plans. While all the girls went off to find a seat, I told them I'd join them later.

After they left, I had a few seconds before I knew our NCO would check the barracks for stragglers. I scanned my room, trying to think on my feet. I desperately didn't want to go, but where could I hide? There was only under the bed, or inside the wardrobe.

Soundlessly, I lifted up the canvas material in front of the wardrobe and slid in, closing it softly. If I stood very straight, to attention, with my arms by my sides, I knew even if someone opened the wardrobe flap they'd not see me!

I waited with baited breath as I heard footsteps. As predicted, it was the NCO checking the rooms.

I heard someone open the door and held my breath in case the canvas flap moved an inch, but thankfully it didn't. I was sure she'd have a fit if she found me. I stood there for what felt like years, until finally I heard footsteps going away again. I waited a while until I heard the girls returning. Sliding neatly out of the wardrobe, I picked up a blanket by the bed and started pretending to fold it.

'Win!' cried Alice. 'Where were you?'

'Oh, just in the wardrobe,' I said casually, laughing at the face she pulled.

'Why didn't you come?' she said.

'I've heard it all before anyway,' I said, waving my hand dismissively. It wasn't true but she didn't need to know that.

Only once did Bertie's past catch up with him. Or, more correctly, it caught up with me.

I was having one of 'those days' this particular afternoon. On the switchboard was someone from Port Said on one line and another officer from Suez on the other. Both were very dodgy lines and as soon as I got a clear line for one, the other one would disappear and vice versa! This went on for a good few minutes and then the line for Port Said froze altogether. I'd already been dying to spend a penny, so decided to leave it and come back. But of course, you can't just walk out. You need someone to cover your line. So I raised my hand.

'I need someone to cover me, please,' I said to the supervisor, a female WAAF called Jeanine. I'd heard a rumour she'd once gone out with Bertie, but I knew better than to ask her.

'Well, you can't,' she replied, rudely. 'You need cover and I don't have anyone to cover you.'

'Could you find someone, please?' I replied. 'I'll not be long.'

'Nope,' she said, sullenly. 'I certainly cannot.'

I stared at her. I'd no idea why she was being so difficult. It didn't make sense to me. Then it occurred perhaps this lady had a chip on her shoulder with me.

I glared at her. 'Are you going to try and find someone or shall I just up and leave my station now?'

'YOU can't do THAT!' she yelled.

That was it then, I was seeing red. Whoever this woman was, she was being very unreasonable.

I picked up my dockets and threw them into the air. Then I went to walk out. But she pushed me hard on the shoulder, causing me almost to lose balance.

'Hey!' I cried in shock.

Instinctively I raised a fist to strike her.

'Do it!' she screamed at me. 'And I'll have you!'

Somehow, I recovered my senses quickly enough to get the hell out of there. I felt really rather shaken. Why was she treating me like this? What was her problem?

I marched smartly to the toilet, to recover myself. Then I just slipped back to the station and kept my head down until the shift was over.

News of our scuffle broke out and everyone wanted to know about it. I just wanted to forget it though. Unfortunately this was easier said than done, as I was charged with affray, my punishment being seven days confined in the barracks. I was gutted! Bertie and I were due to go to Cairo together for a few days.

When I finally told him of the incident his face looked grim.

'That was my ex, Jeanine,' he said. 'And I bet she has a good right hook on her.'

Going away on leave was hard anyway, without the likes of Jeanine putting the mockers on it. If Bertie and I wanted to go to Cairo we had to have a chaperone. It was silly really as if we'd wanted to do anything deemed 'immoral' there was plenty of opportunity on other occasions.

But we had to stick by the rules all the same, so when we did get away, I begged my friend Pauline to come with us. She did so with her boyfriend and the four of us went together to Cairo.

I thought it was an amazing place. So vast and busy! It was so manic, with cars and people and animals everywhere. I loved the small square fronts of the houses and shops, the way everyone seemed so intent on getting somewhere.

We stayed at small hotels, going out for dinner every night somewhere different or having English fare at wherever we were staying. Not everyone welcomed us though.

One day we decided to finally go and see the pyramids, something I'd been longing to do.

On the way there though, Bertie began to look uneasy. He kept glancing into the wing mirror of our cab. Then he tapped the driver on the shoulder and said something in Egyptian.

'Is everything OK?' I whispered.

'We're not going to see the tourist traps anymore,' he muttered.

'Why?' I asked.

He looked behind us briefly at the traffic. 'We're being followed, that's all I am saying.'

It was scary stuff, not knowing who was following us or why. But I just sat tight in the back of the car, squeezed his hand and hoped we'd get to see the pyramids another time.

I saw the dark side of Egypt a few times. Once we were travelling on a bus from Ismalia when Bertie turned to me and pushed my face towards the side window as the bus came skidding to a halt. A big crowd had gathered and a commotion was going on outside.

'Don't look, Phill, don't look!' he ordered.

He leaped out of the bus and of course I did turn my head then. On one side of the road was a young lad's head, covered in blood and clean off his neck. On the other side was his body.

One splinter group of Egyptians was so incensed at our continued presence in their country they often lay booby traps for our lads. This time they'd placed a piece of wire across a street in time for a signals despatch rider. It took his head off as easy as a piece of cheese.

Bertie spent a while trying to sort out an ambulance to take the boy away and took down some witness details. He got back on the bus looking quite ill.

'It's not a nice business,' he said. 'I hope you didn't look.'

The next time we wanted to get away, Bertie hadn't got around to arranging a chaperone and all hell broke loose when the officers found out. So Bertie had to go to his own office and persuade the Sergeant and his wife to come with us, which they did.

At Christmas we went back to Cairo and again saw some big races there, Bertie's favourite. We spotted Rita Hayworth and Aly Khan looking glamorous in the crowd too. It was so much fun, but then it always was, being with Bertie.

A few weeks before the end of our two-year stint, one final terrifying adventure was to occur. I was having a day off and had planned a luxurious day lounging on the sandy beach, sunbathing. It couldn't have been better weather for it.

I got up and into my bikini but as I looked out the window, something seemed strange. I couldn't put my finger on it but the atmosphere outside was incredibly eerie. Everything suddenly seemed to go very quiet. The wind seemed to disappear and not a tree or a leaf stirred.

What's going on? I thought.

It felt like the very air I was breathing had changed. The atmosphere made the hairs on my neck tingle. Before I could get ready to go and catch the bus, I stepped outside, but the sun seemed to disappear behind a strange mist.

A whooshing sound filled the air, almost as if the sky was moaning, and then swirls and swirls of sand lifted up and everything turned grey. I ran like a hunted rabbit into my quarters and slammed the door shut; most of the other girls had already made it inside.

We stood by the window, watching the whole scene outside turn to a grey, sandy colour, as men and women ran for cover. Our ceiling kept rising and falling too, as if it was about to break.

Alice pointed at it, her face full of worry. 'Do you think it'll cave in, Win?' she asked.

I tried to laugh it off. 'Course not, Alice!' I joked. But inside I wondered the same.

The sound of the storm grew into a screaming crescendo. It was almost maddening. At the time it felt like it was going to last forever as the sandstorm went on for two whole days. Sand could get into the tiniest gap and even with the doors and windows firmly shut everything was coated in the stuff. We quickly grew quite sick of it.

It made keeping our rooms and beds in that apple pie order even more hard work. The NCO always came every morning to do room inspection, and then she'd write on our 'daily inspection card' how we were doing. I nearly always got a 'very good' but after the storm, for some reason, we couldn't seem to get rid of the sand. We had no vacuum cleaners so it was all back-breaking brush and dustpan work.

For the next day she wrote 'dusty' on my form. I thought this was very unfair. So I wrote something rude beside it, which didn't impress my NCO, but I'd made my point.

The poor cooks had a dreadful time and were doing their best, trying to cook everything under muslin, but of course everything was coated in even more sand. I didn't eat for days after the storm. Every single meal was full of gritty sand that got stuck in the crevices of your teeth and in your throat.

During my medical before we were sent home the doctor was shocked at the weight I'd lost. 'Don't stand on a grate sideways or we'll lose you,' he joked, grabbing hold of the top of my skinny little arm. Even with Bertie feeding me up, I'd reached just seven stone.

Chapter Eleven

Back to Blighty

All too soon, the two years were over and it was time to go back. I was gutted to be leaving and would've liked to have stayed on but we had to do as we were told. Occasionally some of the women would complain about the decisions made on their behalf. Some would even threaten to go and tell our MPs if we weren't stationed where we wanted to be! But of course no one ever did. You did what you were told, and you always knew it would come to an end sooner or later.

I never had a big conversation with Bertie about what would happen, or our future. As we said goodbye, he wrapped his arms around me.

'I will see you so very soon, Phill,' he said.

I smiled. I didn't doubt he would.

Then, in March 1951, we boarded a troop ship called the *Fowey*, and were on our way back to England. The sea was very rough all the way home and our poor Sergeant was as sick as a dog. We had to look after her, making sure she was drinking water and not dehydrating. In fact most of the girls were ill on the way back. For some strange reason the rocking of the ship didn't affect me one little bit, so I made the most of the free extra portions and empty rooms. I even went to bingo one evening and found I was the only one there. And of course the bar was empty night after night, so I didn't have to queue for a drink.

'Your guts must be made of steel,' the girls joked, sounding a tad jealous.

On board our ship were some lads returning from the war in Korea and many of them were wounded. They were kept separately from us, although we did pass them in corridors.

I bumped into one lad and it was quite an unpleasant experience.

He was only about nineteen and was looking around anxiously.

'Please help me!' he begged me. 'I need to send a telegram to my mum.'

'What about?' I asked, concerned.

'She's been told that I'm dead,' he explained. 'I need to tell her I am alive and it was a mistake and I am coming home. Can you do it for me?'

I looked at him in horror.

'No way!' I cried. 'The shock of reading that might kill her!'

There was something about this lad I didn't like. I didn't know if he was telling the truth or just trying to get attention from me but I wanted no part of it.

'If you want someone to do it,' I said, 'find someone else.' And I quickly walked off.

The trip home was very different from the sense of excitement and anticipation on the way out. We were segregated into classes and there were no ports of call apart from a quick stop at Gibraltar to pick up some prisoners (who were actually soldiers who'd been very naughty for one reason or another).

Even the views were different as we were surrounded by thick, soup-like, grey fog, and with the waves being so rough it wasn't an easy trip. It seemed to go on for ever.

Finally though, we woke one morning to hear the anchor being paid out just off the Isle of Wight. We had to wait there all day as no berth was available in Southampton until the evening. As it was dark when we arrived we had to wait until next morning to disembark. On deck I could hear music playing and on the shore were bands playing with lots of people waving and shouting. They were families waiting for their loved ones back from Korea.

Some of the soldiers were allowed on shore that evening and we watched as wives, girlfriends, parents and children threw their arms around their loved ones. It was very moving to see.

That night felt like a long one. We were all tired and just itching to be on our way home now, after such a long time away and a long journey. Many of us couldn't sleep and we were up and ready before daylight, just desperate to get off the damned ship and get home.

After a final breakfast we waited patiently for our kit and were ferried to the customs. I hadn't reckoned on this part of the trip and actually, even though we were service personnel, they were as rigorous as ever . . . quite an unnerving prospect when you didn't have much money on you to pay for things you'd bought.

We had to wait for the customs officer to eyeball our things and quiz us on what we were bringing into the country. I was rather shaky when he turned to me, as he'd made some people pay up extra or leave their things behind.

'I've just got twenty pounds' worth of food and chocolate for my brother and wife,' I babbled.

The customs man laughed. 'That's fine, bring in as much food as you like,' he said. 'Have you got any valuables like watches, cigarettes or spirits?' he asked.

I clamped my hand over the watch Bertie had given me. It was a beautiful gift but I had no extra money to pay duty on it.

'You'll have to pay for that,' he said, eyeing my wrist.

I could feel myself filling up in my eyes. 'I honestly cannot part with this,' I said. 'But I can't afford the duty either.'

Fortunately he didn't seem to be in the mood to argue and waved me through. I wore that watch for many years afterwards.

After another tedious trip to Brighton for our railway warrants, I had to get a train to London, standing all the way because lots of sailors were travelling too.

Getting off at London was an eye-opener. Everywhere I looked there seemed to be many colours of skin, far more than when I'd left. There were lots of Asian and Jamaican faces and I thought the station and streets seemed busier than ever.

* * *

My journey was far from over though and I had to get another train from London to Norwich. By then I was absolutely exhausted and found myself falling asleep on my feet, until I woke, face down in someone's smelly kit bag. Thankfully some sailors saw I needed help and half-carried me off the train to get my connection. They practically threw me and my kit onto the next train to Yarmouth just as it was pulling out, but I couldn't have been more grateful. I was totally washed out by now.

At Yarmouth it was the final leg and a taxi to Ken's house. I managed to jump in with some people who quizzed me on where I was coming home from.

'Egypt,' I sighed, to their surprise. 'I've been serving abroad for two years.'

They weren't expecting that response and insisted on paying my part of the fare.

It was 10.15 p.m. when I arrived and Ken was just coming out of his flat to walk the dog when I almost fell out of the cab in front of his front door.

He dashed back in and called Phyllis, who emerged crying, as Ken went to get me some brandy.

'Win,' he said, helping me up to the bedroom, 'you look so ill.' He gave me the glass. 'Drink some of this!'

Before long my head hit the pillow and I fell soundly asleep. I woke a few hours later to find Ken by my side. 'Are you OK?' he asked, anxiously.

'Yes, I'm fine,' I replied. 'I've just lost a little weight.'

Later that day, after I'd managed to eat a good breakfast, Phyllis told me why she'd been crying.

'You're so thin,' she said. 'We thought you must be really ill!'

I managed to laugh now. 'No,' I told her, 'the food in Egypt was horrible and it just took a very, very long time to get back home.'

It didn't take me long to relax and put on a bit of weight with some good dinners and teas inside me. I also gave up smoking. Most people smoked in those days, but I felt I should try and give up, especially as I thought it might help me put on weight.

While I was staying at Ken's a submarine was reported to have sunk just off Portland and I thought of poor Betty again. It was so sad. Such dangerous work, and what a terrible way to end your life, trapped so far below all humanity. I didn't know what was to happen to me next, but the army soon decided. I got a letter saying I was being posted to Grays in Essex. I was to report to the Signal Regiment at Orsett Camp the following week.

So before long I was off again, but this time I dropped in to visit my family in Canterbury en route. I had to get the ferry across from Essex to Kent to meet Maisie and her mother-in-law. As I stood on deck, it felt lovely to have the familiar sights come into view.

We spent a wonderful day together catching up. Afterwards Maisie told me how her mother-in-law had said, 'Look, there's Winifred Phillips at the door in her uniform.' I'd no idea how she'd recognised me. They'd not even seen me for a couple of years by now.

Mum's Army

I enjoyed reconnecting with them. I had my brothers, but my auntie's family were always so welcoming and I vowed to make more effort to keep in touch with them.

Although I reported to the base in Essex I was to be stationed in Stanmore this time, back on the switchboard. Then I was sent to nearby Bushey Heath in Hertfordshire, where the WRAC were living in a large old house.

Our place of work was a few minutes' walk away, but ultimately we were left to our own devices in this house. It was an incredibly old rambling place with a bell tower on the roof. The temptation was too much for us, and we'd crawl on top of it to do a spot of sunbathing and tease each other about trying to get the bell going. It also had a huge garden and was like something out of a fairy story, now all badly overgrown.

Watford town centre was just a bus ride away, and it was a fabulous place to go shopping (although we still couldn't afford an awful lot).

The only fly in the ointment of this lovely time was when our officer would come over from a nearby camp and subject us to a rigorous inspection.

She was a Major, and we called her 'Old Gildy' (well, some less polite people did). I didn't actually mind her at all. She was only doing her job. But it was hard to get through her inspections sometimes.

We'd hear a rap on the door and then with a grim face she'd set about pulling our house apart, looking for untidy drawers, cupboards or a layer of dust we'd missed.

We always kept the house shipshape, but still she'd find something.

'What do you think THIS is?' she'd shout, pulling a slightly stained teaspoon from the cutlery drawer.

We'd be on eggshells throughout her visit.

Once I came home later from a shift to hear Old Gildy had just been on a visit. One of the girls was clearing up the kitchen, and there was some kind of sticky substance on the floor when I arrived.

'What's that, Jenny?' I asked.

Jenny looked up; her face told me she'd been laughing hysterically and she began again now.

'It's Old Gildy,' she howled. 'You'll never guess what happened . . .'

Apparently Old Gildy had shown up, in as foul a mood as ever, and set upon the kitchen in her usual robust manner. This time she'd focused on the top of the kitchen cupboards.

She started pulling at any items she could see, and then she found a giant tin of jam we'd kept up there. In a fit of temper, unable to pull it down, she gave it a good jerk and the whole lot tumbled onto her head, the lid coming off and thick red strawberry jam drooling onto her head in a sticky mess.

I started laughing loudly, as Jenny carried on. 'She started clawing at her hair, her fingers getting all stuck in the jam, and it dribbled down her face into her eyes . . . Oh, Phill, it was the hardest thing in the world not to laugh out loud in front of her.'

I was sorry I'd missed such a spectacle, but equally glad I'd not had to try and contain myself.

Mum's Army

My first job at this post was to clean up the switchboard, which until now had been run by some men. I was appalled at the state of it. It was filthy! Full of crumbs, fingerprints, leftover cups of tea and bits of biscuit. I realised then the women ran a much tighter ship when it came to switchboard hygiene.

It was at my Stanmore posting I met a lovely woman called Joan, who had the most beautiful dark hair I'd ever seen. Even though she was my supervisor, we got on very well and she went on to become a very dear friend. We had to hide our friendship, as I didn't want people to think she was favouring me.

She obviously did respect my work though, and when she was off she decided to put me in charge. Even though I could be cheeky sometimes, I always worked very hard and it felt good to have this recognised.

That morning as I sat in the supervisor's chair, some of the girls were shocked to see me in charge.

'Why are you in charge? You're too young,' barked one of them. 'You only look about seventeen!'

'I am not!' I cried. 'Guess how old I am?'

They couldn't believe I was twenty-seven. I'd always looked more youthful I suppose.

As promised, I'd kept in touch with Bertie and was looking forward to him coming to visit me on his leave.

He came down and I met him at the station. He looked so brown from the sun. I could already barely remember what it felt like to have a tan.

'Lovely to see you, Win,' he said, hugging me at the station.

Because we weren't married he had to stay at a B&B in a pub nearby until we decided to go away for a few days to Devon. Of course, we went round some horse and car races. I loved being with Bertie as he was always so keen on walking around and taking in the world. Then he had some news.

'I've got another posting, I'm not sure where,' he said. 'But it won't be in this country.'

We didn't discuss it further. His career was important to him, as mine was to me, and I knew without a doubt he'd go.

I just got on with it and tried to put it to the back of my mind, just enjoying things as they happened.

A few weeks after his visit, I got a letter from him. 'Sorry, Phill, but it's over between us,' he wrote.

There was no explanation. Nothing. Even though I sensed from the start that Bertie and me wouldn't be for ever, I was devastated, and sat for a while with the letter in my hand. I felt so heavy with sadness and upset. A few days later, I heard from one of the girls that Bertie had become friendly with the daughter of another officer. Eventually this all went wrong and Bertie found himself sent back home.

There was more upset when I heard from Betty too, with whom I'd kept in touch via letters. Her life had taken a terrible twist. It *was* her husband's sub that had sunk, on his last mission . . . and just after she'd found out that she was pregnant and expecting twins. My heart just went out to her and it reminded me again what a dangerous career we'd chosen.

Between 1951 and 1955, I was promoted to Sergeant and it felt like a big step up.

Now I had extra duties of supervising people but, best of all, I got to stay in the Sergeants' mess. It depended where you were, but you always had more room and they were usually far nicer areas to stay in. You often got a room to share with just one or two others, instead of all being piled into one big room.

As a Sergeant, I also had to take drill, which meant barking orders at the squad during their marches. It didn't bother me one bit doing this, as I'd had it done to me, and I was keen to step up the ranks.

We also had drill competitions when away at summer camp, which both myself and Joan had teams of people doing. A drill is where you get your squad and you teach them to march and preside over it.

I had to shout: 'Left, right, left, right . . .' and then 'eyes to left, eyes to right . . .' and so on. It was hard going and we really had to be strict, especially with the dress code. The ladies' skirts had to be exactly the right length above the knee but also while they stood next to each other they had to be the same length . . . quite a tricky business when you had ladies of different heights. I'd get out my ruler before they set off and measure them one by one. Then it was time to drill them and put them on parade. During the drill, they had to listen to my orders and do whatever I asked in synch. Not a mean feat for some of the newbies.

One month I won the cup for the drill. There were three squads taking part, one from the regiment in Grays, and one from each detachment at Bushey Heath and Knightsbridge.

I had a host of other duties too, including things like being responsible for discipline. For example if someone came back late from leave I'd have to pull them up on it and get them to report to the office in the morning for a dressing-down.

There was very little difference between Sergeant and Staff Sergeant duties. In fact, the only difference I could ever see was the small crown above the stripes we stitched onto our sleeves.

Once I'd become more experienced and climbed to this rank, I could tell that women joined the army from all walks of life and it didn't take a certain 'type' of woman to want to sign up. But one thing we did all have in common was discipline. None of us shied away from it and, on the whole, we were all hard workers.

As always, drama was never far away from camp and even in Essex it was no exception.

Once, when over there for a regimental weekend, I woke to find the place swarming with police officers.

'What on earth has happened?' I asked Joan.

'There's been a murder!' she said.

'A murder!'

It sounded like something out of a horror film, but an old man had been attacked alongside his wife in the house next door to the barracks.

Mum's Army

One of the lads had been painting fire buckets that morning and police had nabbed him when they spotted him with his hands coated in red paint! After a few enquiries they soon discovered they were barking up the wrong tree and eventually a soldier who'd been demobbed was arrested. He'd stabbed the poor old man in a bungled robbery apparently.

I was horrified. But once again, it showed me you never knew what was around the corner.

Chapter Twelve

Running the Show

As my friendship with Joan deepened she introduced me to her fiancé, Andy, a serious, dark-haired man she'd met on a boat trip in Hong Kong when she was stationed there. I became firm friends with both of them.

We spent time over dinners and loved working together – Joan and I were both Sergeants now. Every year we were also sent away to 'camp'; this was supposed to be a sort of team-building exercise, and supposedly a bit of a 'holiday' for us, although I never saw it like that! One year we went away to Aberporth, Wales, and we were given a bunch of Z-list reservists to take with us.

Joan and myself and a hundred reservists . . . when I saw this command, I turned to her and said, 'What are we supposed to do with this lot?' It seemed like a big task to take on!

Z-listers were old army boys who'd done their service but because of their abilities were put on a register, so they could be called up in times of trouble. Many were called up in Korea to back up the regular troops. Every so often they took part in exercises, to keep their abilities fresh.

We arrived in the camp to find it was at a 'rocket' station. It was basically a damp concrete bunker and quite hideous to sleep in.

After we arrived, I ordered everyone to unpack their clothes and set up the barrack room. But as I unfolded my things, my ears were filled with a sound I'll never forget.

Whoooooooooomph!

My chest reverberated and my ears rang as I ran like a trembling jelly into my neighbour's room. I found myself wrapped around the nearest female, my arms and legs clinging on for dear life. It was absolutely terrifying. Losing all control, I started sobbing like a baby.

'Wh-wh-what was that?' I screamed. It felt as if the world was about to end.

Joan came rushing in. 'Phill, there's a rocket station next door to us too,' she said. 'Didn't you realise?'

Without any warning the lads at the station had let a practice rocket off next door.

'But they didn't tell us!' I cried, trying to recover my dignity. I soon found out they usually sounded a whistle before setting off a rocket to warn people, but I hadn't noticed one this time.

We had some old telephone exchanges and were told we had to train the reservists up to use them. 'That will be easier said than done,' I moaned.

But actually many of the boys were old hands. They'd all fought in the Second World War and actually knew how to use these types of machinery better than we did.

'You make this job look easy,' I laughed, as they nimbly took over the switchboard.

We had to give them lectures and show them the ropes, brushing up their skills, half of them would say: 'We know that, we taught you that . . .'

Dealing with some of them was a bit like herding cats, as often one or two would go missing. We'd count up the numbers and then have to go off looking for them. A few times I found men up on the cliff sunbathing.

'What do you think you're up to?' I barked at them.

'Having a holiday,' they quipped, squinting in the sun. In their view the government had sent them on camp for a holiday too, and that's what they were determined to have.

The story of my rocket fright had apparently reached the rest of the reservists . . . as I soon found out during one of my classes. I was just giving another lesson about the exchange, when I was distracted by a buzzing noise.

'What's that?' I gasped, looking up from my notes.

A straight-faced reservist looked at me. 'It must just be a rocket launch about to take place,' he said. 'Maybe we should all just sit down and wait until it's over.'

I almost dropped my notes in a rush to take a seat and put my fingers in my ears. No way did I wish to get caught out like last time. We waited for several minutes in silence, as the buzzing continued. I was just wishing it would hurry up and be over, when one of the men pointed at his watch.

'Ma'am, it's time for a NAAFI break,' he said. 'Can we go?'

'Not until after this launch,' I whispered loudly, tight with anticipation.

It was then the room broke up with laughter. 'Oh, but ma'am, there is no launch, we've been pulling your leg, it's Brian's watch . . .'

I looked up to see a reservist tapping his watch, which was duly making the ominous buzzing sound.

'What!' I cried.

They were all rolling with laughter as they got up one by one to leave for their break. I couldn't say anything – sometimes it's best to go along with the joke, whatever it is.

Around this time, I was posted to Knightsbridge for three years. There were many of us, all from different regiments, and I was there as duty officer to represent the signals in the ack-ack squad. If you'd asked me what the point of the ack-ack regiment was, I'd have struggled to give an answer. The term ack-ack is short for anti-aircraft fire, and there were stations set up all over the country during the war. They carried on into the 1950s but the units were wound up soon afterwards.

I loved my time at Knightsbridge. We had a lovely flat to stay in and it was quite a doddle as jobs go. I became firm friends with Billie, a personal assistant to General Fanshaw in Rutland Gate. We used to go dancing together every night we could, along with plenty of others including a fun chap called Cedric Grimshaw. Cedric was so much fun, always game for a laugh and wanting to crack a joke and have a drink with us.

The best thing about Knightsbridge was being away from the regiment and not having to follow all the strict rules. I had fun where I could, as I didn't have to face the music with all my superiors being back in Essex.

I was always the person they called upon to do the errand-type jobs and a bit of this and that, like laying the wreath on Remembrance Day or attending meetings at the Union Jack club, a private members' club for personnel and ex-personnel that's still very popular today. If anything ever needed doing in London it was always a case of: 'Ask Phill'.

One of the jobs suddenly thrust upon me was to check the despatch riders had all the right tools to fix their bikes. I had to inspect them and then make a list of things that were missing. But I had absolutely no clue what to do!

So for a joke, instead of writing a note of the mechanical tools missing, I grabbed a whole range of things instead, like a tin opener, an old door key, a window key, etc., and then put them in the box and sent them to the regiment with a note saying: 'Please replace these items.'

I was told afterwards the quartermaster in Essex almost had a fit. He told the despatch: 'Your Sergeant has got a bloody cheek. But for her cheek I'll give her some new ones anyway.'

My social life really took off in Knightsbridge too. There were plenty of boys around to take us out and most evenings we went to the West End. It was a lovely place in those days, you could walk for miles, just looking at the bars and soaking up the jovial, exciting atmosphere of areas around Hyde Park and Sloane Square. Although it was always bustling it was quite a peaceful place, with everyone just rather cheerful and friendly. We didn't often go dancing though, we usually just met in a pub or went for moonlit walks around Hyde Park.

We often spotted the old Chelsea Pensioners too, wandering around, resplendent in their scarlet coats. They were some of the 300 veterans who'd gained a prestigious place to live out their days in peace in the Royal Hospital, a beautiful building near Sloane Square, originally designed by Sir Christopher Wren, who'd built St Paul's Cathedral.

I often walked past it, gazing up at the astonishing building, imagining what it would be like to live there. I knew it was only for old boys, but I somehow felt like maybe I'd end up there myself.

Although I loved London, we were there during the Great Smog in December 1952. This was when fog mixed with air pollutants like car exhausts and chimney smoke to form a terrible dense thick fog around the capital. Times like this were called 'pea-soupers' as it was like walking around in a bowl of it.

Sometimes it would come down right in the middle of the day. One Sunday around 1 p.m. we'd just had lunch when it descended.

'Quick, look at this,' shouted Billie, as we started putting on the lights even thought it was early afternoon.

We looked out of the door and saw ominous swirls of grey rolling in. It really was quite frightening. Then we heard some screams and cries coming from Hyde Park. We opened the door and stuck out our heads.

'Oh my golly,' I said. 'Listen to them!'

People, tourists probably, were literally shouting for help. They'd got completely lost as the fog had suddenly descended without warning. It must've been most disorientating.

'God save us!' one cried.

'Dear God, please save our souls, help us, please!' another sobbed.

We couldn't see them but we could hear them.

'You'll be OK!' yelled Billie. 'It's just smog.'

We closed the window to stop it from coming in and looked at each other.

'I feel so sorry for them, but you can't see your hand in front of your face,' said Billie.

On other nights we heard of terrible car crashes and pedestrians being mown down. In the end all public transport stopped and even ambulances stopped coming to emergencies. It was like walking around blind.

The newspapers said the cause was due to the incredibly cold weather causing more people to burn coal, on top of the coal-burning power stations and poor weather conditions; London's air became a choking cauldron.

I always avoided it and stayed in when it came down. The smell was a horrible, acrid stench and it made your eyes water and hairs in the nostril burn. Many people found it hard to breathe too and hospitals were filled with people sometimes dying.

I saw for myself how fast it could come down when I was on a train going from London to Fareham when the smog suddenly rolled in. It was white fog at first but gradually changed colour to dark grey. It was horrible, very eerie.

Our love lives always kept us busy though. I was dating a policeman at this point – another Harry. Again, it wasn't something I took particularly seriously, but it was nice to go out dancing and have someone to look out for me. In fact I ended up being witness at his wedding!

Billie ended up marrying the ADC (aide de camp – a personal assistant to someone of high rank) of the General she was looking after. Back then, I'd no idea how demanding the job of PA was. I knew she had to get up at night sometimes, and she often complained of being tired. But it wasn't until years later, and I was a PA myself, I realised how hard it could be!

The Sergeant Major, a quiet woman called Margery, was going out with another Sergeant. She kept it a bit secret, sneaking off for drinks with him and things without letting us know, except we all did know. It was a very serious relationship and we expected them to marry.

Then I heard from someone she'd booked a register office wedding.

'But she doesn't want a soul to know,' said my source. 'She's adamant it must be done in secret.'

'Where is it?' I asked cheekily. Somehow or other I got the information and the date and time of the wedding. It was to be at Victoria.

'Right,' I said to my friends. 'I think we should all go!'

I told everyone quietly and it even filtered up to the officers. Then on the big day, we all got smartly dressed in our uniforms and caught a bus down in time for the happy couple to emerge.

The look on her face was more than blushing bride when she walked out with her new husband, and we all shouted: 'Surprise!'

Poor shy Margery didn't know where to look. But I think she was pleased we'd come after all.

Where our flat was positioned meant we were sometimes privy to the 'other' side of London too. One day I looked out of our flat window to see some finely dressed ladies standing on the edge of Hyde Park. They all wore different colours, one in a grey two-piece, another in beautiful red velvet, another in green, a real sight to behold.

'Look at this, quick!' I said to one of the girls. We pressed our faces up to the window and watched as a gentleman would walk past, briefly speak to one of the girls and then take her on his arm and walk off briskly.

'Oh my,' gasped Sylvia. 'They are prostitutes, Phill!'

From then on we noticed them every evening, arriving just after dusk to ply their trade. We nicknamed them according to the colour of their clothing.

A few weeks later, we heard police sirens and coppers jumping out of cars as the girls ran off into Hyde Park.

'Go on, Greeny!' we shouted, as the girl in the green suit ran as fast as her heels would carry her, outrunning the policemen.

We all cheered them on, hoping they'd get away. I felt sorry for the girls; they must've been in a desperate position to be doing that for a living.

There was a firm group of us who loved to hang around together. Billie and I would always have brandy and lemonade when we were out. This was my tipple. I usually stopped at two and it never occurred to me to drink more. Nobody got drunk very often. We all had jobs to do and it was seen as a bit silly to get 'tight', especially when we had to get up in the morning.

We all proudly wore a funny little red-barrel 'bracelet' around our wrists back then. They were given away by Watneys brewery as part of the promotion for their Red Barrel export pale ale, which was actually the first ever keg beer and very trendy at the time; we were all rather proud of them.

I had a few strange jobs to carry out too. Once, our officer agreed to help with a radio show in Earls Court. This was the age of radio, with comedians such as the Goons taking over the airwaves. Our show was a regular exhibition where singers and dancers and all kinds of things weird and wonderful were displayed to the public to entertain them, and we were going to show off our switchboards. I wasn't sure why the army had agreed to it but went along with orders anyhow. Personally though, I never had time to listen to the radio. When I was off duty, I went out dancing.

Funnily enough, years and years later I ended up giving my identity card for this show to the WRAC museum, something I never would have imagined anyone would be interested in!

I found it hard work, as it was my job to organise the girls and get everyone there and back and make sure it all ran smoothly. One evening I was on my way back when something most unpleasant happened on the train.

A man started shouting and cussing me. He was screaming about women shouldn't be allowed to be in the armed forces, and he started waving his hands in my face, and kicking my bag.

'Who do you think you are?' he screamed. 'Being in the army and wearing a skirt!'

I recoiled into my seat, really scared for myself. But luckily people quickly stepped in and he was thrown off the train at the next stop.

'Are you all right?' a passing gentleman asked.

'Yes, thank you,' I said, pushing a strand of hair from my face.

I'd no idea what the man's objection to women in the army was, but it gave me quite a fright. I rushed back to the safety of the barracks afterwards, making sure nobody was following me. I told a police officer on duty near the camp about it.

'It scared the living daylights out of me,' I admitted.

'Right,' he said. 'I will meet you off that train every evening from now on.' And he did. It was so kind of him.

Chapter Thirteen

Crowning Glory

While I was in Knightsbridge, staying in Rutland Gate, the coronation of our new Queen took place in 1953 and it was all terribly exciting. Boys from the signals were taking part in the parade, as were troops from all over the country. It was a time of great pride.

I'd already heard stories about the Princess Elizabeth and her time in the ATS. She was the same age as me and had joined up just before the end of the war, although I doubted she'd have had to get her hands dirty very often.

Some of the girls I met over the years told me stories about when she'd stayed at their barracks.

'She was often seen driving a lorry,' said one girl.

'She'd only drive cars,' countered another. 'She wasn't allowed anywhere near a lorry.'

'She was very well protected,' claimed someone else. 'She had secret service with her everywhere and she never had to pitch in like the rest of us.'

Once I read a story about her in the newspaper, saying how she'd cleaned cars like all the other women, but I wasn't sure what to believe in the end, quite honestly! I expect she was very well looked after and didn't have quite the same treatment as the rest of us. I also imagined she probably hated it. Well, she was royalty!

In our mess, I was sharing a room with a lovely girl called Sylvia at this time, and I set my alarm the night before the coronation to have plenty of time to get ready.

That evening, Sylvia was standing by our balcony and kept bobbing her head out of the window.

'What are you up to?' I asked.

'Eating grapes,' she sniggered. I peered over the balcony and watched as she spat the pips out of the window onto some cars below.

'Who do they belong to?' I asked, realising she was doing it on purpose.

'The German Embassy next door,' she laughed. 'A man's been washing them all afternoon for the big day tomorrow.'

I half-laughed. 'You're getting away with murder,' I said.

The next morning, my alarm went off all too soon and I leaped out of bed to get ready. We were all spending the day in the Sergeants' mess to watch the TV set in there and eat nibbles.

'Can't believe it's seven o'clock already,' I yawned, as Sylvia pottered around getting dressed.

'Come on, then,' she said. 'Let's go for an early walk around before the big day starts.'

Sylvia was always nagging me to go for walks with her, but I was usually too busy. I'd come up with an excuse as I always liked to have plenty of time to get ready in the morning, but this time I agreed to go on a quick walk.

Mum's Army

We had a wander around Hyde Park, watching people putting up bunting and feeling an air of excitement rise. There were hundreds of people all camping out in The Mall for a good spot in the procession. Even though it had rained the night before, nothing could dampen their cheer and excitement.

On our way I glanced at a church clock. 'Hey, it's only seven o'clock now,' I complained.

Sylvia laughed. 'I put your alarm clock an hour forward just to make sure you had time for bit of fresh air first,' she admitted.

I could've swung for her!

We eventually made our way down to the packed mess, and everyone drew up chairs and settled down to watch.

Elizabeth looked beautiful and I had no doubt she'd make a terrific Queen. There was something so quietly confident and calm about her. Then we watched some officers we knew lead our regiment among all the other troops proudly marching past. I got a real shiver down my spine, thinking what an honour this all was.

After we saw them on TV, we rushed to the street outside to watch the procession march past in real life too. It was such fanfare, so many bright colours, flags, and pomp and ceremony. I must admit I had my heart in my mouth as they went by. I always felt nervous when royalty were out and about; after all, anything could happen, like assassination attempts and so on. And there was something about the sense of tradition and pomp I shied away from. But also you could breathe in the air filled with a sense of history and occasion.

Later Sylvia insisted we make our way down to Buckingham Palace to see our newly crowned Queen wave to her people from the balcony in the evening.

'Go on, Phill,' she chided. 'It'll be worth it.'

Golly, I decided I'd never do anything like it again when I found myself squashed like a sardine up against thousands of people around us. The noise was deafening, with people cheering and screaming. The overriding feeling was one of joy, but I couldn't help but sense some hysteria too.

'People aren't going to get a better view by pushing,' I hissed, hinting at the women behind me.

Sylvia kept digging me in the back, to push me further forward too.

'Exciting, isn't it, Win?' she beamed.

'Yes, yes,' I said, not wanting to appear a killjoy.

I ended up in the armpit of the poor lady standing in front of me.

But what would you know – when she turned around to ask me to give her some room I recognised the face.

'Do you mind?' she said, shoving me backwards.

'Oh my!' I gasped. 'You worked in the quartermaster store in Egypt!' We both laughed. It's such a small world sometimes.

The crowd roared as Elizabeth finally did make an appearance, and the atmosphere was electric. But as soon as she disappeared, I turned to Sylvia and started pushing my way out.

'Right, I want to get back for a nice cup of tea,' I said. 'And you're making it!'

It took us hours and hours to walk back home, even though it wasn't far, there were so many people wandering around. I felt half-dead and was gasping for a cuppa by the time we returned. 'Never again,' I said, rubbing my feet.

Whatever we were doing we always looked absolutely smart at all times, especially in this camp in Knightsbridge. I must admit I was very good at this. I always had the correct uniform and didn't mind giving things a good iron. Being well turned out had become as natural as breathing to me.

I think it was particularly expected in Knightsbridge as it was such a posh area and we were 'seen' by many VIPs. Lots of royals had friends in the area and big expensive cars were constantly rolling up and down the roads, with well-dressed types pitching in and out.

Once I spotted a lady emerging from a car wearing the most fancy and beautiful-looking hat I'd ever seen. I was literally in awe of it and found myself stopping dead in the street just to gaze at it. Full of feathers and made of velvet, it seemed to glow in the spot of sunshine that day. As I only ever had my uniform to wear, I often found myself admiring other civvies' pretty clothes with something akin to envy.

Suddenly though, she turned her head and gave me a rather steely look. I quickly looked away, as if I'd been caught touching her hat and not just looking at it. My heart quickened as she pointed at me and walked towards me.

Oh, Win, you're for it now, I thought, my palms sweating. I imagined I'd be getting a telling-off for staring at her. This lady with the hat, whoever she was, had a bit of status, that much was obvious.

'Come here, please,' she said.

I marched smartly over. 'Yes, madam,' I said politely.

'How long have you got left in the army?' she asked.

I was a little taken aback by her question.

'Erm,' I said, 'I'm not sure.' The real answer was probably about ten years.

'What are you going to do when you get out?' she went on.

Now I really was confused.

'I have no idea,' I said.

'Well,' she replied, looking me up and down carefully. 'My husband is the Governor of Tasmania and if you're needing a job just get in touch with me and I will give you one. You're looking very smart . . .' And with that she turned on her clippy-clop heels and with a nod of her hat she was gone.

I looked on mesmerised. I'd absolutely no idea where Tasmania even was, let alone had any desire to work there, but I was chuffed all the same.

That was the thing in those days, you could get offered a job just by walking down the street, and I knew it was a genuine offer too. But I wasn't in a rush to take her up on it. I had other plans . . .

After three years in Knightsbridge, I had my eye on where to go next. The ack-ack group was being wound up now and so we all had to move on anyway. In peacetime there was no need for such a regiment, originally set up to specialise in anti-aircraft fire to be dotted around the country, 'just in case'; I was never quite sure of our role anyway, but now especially so.

So the next thing I needed to find out was where I'd be going next. And I already had my heart set on a certain beautiful country I'd heard all about through Joan . . . Singapore.

By now I'd become firm friends with both Joan and Andy and they were due to get married over there the following year.

Joan had asked me to be her bridesmaid. I said I'd be honoured, but only if I could somehow get out there! I knew if I didn't get a posting I'd not make it.

Fortunately, I'd also made an effort to get to know the man who made these decisions. I never met Sidney, who worked in the records office, but always took time to chat to him on the switchboard.

This time I needed his help. With a bit of front I rang him up for a private chat.

'You know where I'd really, really like to go next?' I slipped in, halfway through the conversation.

'Where is that then, Phillips?' he asked.

'Singapore,' I sighed. I knew I wasn't being in the slightest bit subtle about this, but I didn't care. I just hoped it worked.

We talked for a bit more and then I put down the phone, keeping my fingers crossed.

As it turned out, my chat with Sidney appeared to work and there was a place for me to go to Singapore, but not as a Staff Sergeant, only as a Sergeant. So I happily 'demoted' myself, much to the surprise of others. It was still a role as a supervisor and there was little difference in the job I'd be doing.

Before I could go to Singapore though, I had one last hurdle. For some reason I needed some insurance documents as part of my signing up.

'Are you sure?' I quizzed the officer when he told me.

He nodded, his face resolute, and my heart sank a little. I wanted to pretend I didn't know where these documents were, but I knew exactly where I'd left them. At my father's house. And there was only one way of getting hold of them; contacting him again.

I sent a letter to Dad, my first correspondence with him in around seven years. He wrote back immediately, inviting me to come and stay with him and, of course, Olive.

I felt very reluctant but decided all I needed to do was go, turn up with a smile plastered on my face, get what I needed and leave again. I didn't relish having to reconnect with either of them.

Dad came to meet me at Leamington station and we had an awkward handshake of a 'hello'. Olive was there by his side, her smile fake, which was very evident to me. If I'd had my way I would've grabbed the document there and then and walked off, but I had to go home for a few days.

My heart just felt very hard the whole time, as I sat through meal after meal, making small talk. I realised then, I really did feel almost nothing for my father. He was just a man to me, not a dad in any sense of the word. I didn't even feel sad about this by now. I just wanted to get back in with the girls and be on my way.

One good thing was that he'd invited all my brothers down to come and see me off. It was so lovely to have Norman, Ken and Cliff around me again. The house wasn't big enough for us all to sit around a table, so we sat with cups of tea on the couch and had a bit of a catch-up.

The boys had all been in the army by now, even Cliff. He'd joined up at nineteen but had suffered from pneumonia. While in hospital a doctor had broken a needle inside his back during treatment and poor Cliff (always in the wars) ended up very ill and in hospital for a whole year. He was medically discharged after that.

My dad wasn't interested in my new career, really. He still didn't approve and never asked me anything about it.

As Dad said goodbye, we had another slightly awkward hug.

'Come and see us again soon, Win,' he said.

I smiled politely but inside thought, not likely.

To reach Singapore we had to sail for twenty-eight days. This time it was to be on the troop ship *Lancashire* and to be honest it was nothing short of a holiday. We sailed down the Suez Canal at night-time, and I was a little sad as I couldn't see anything of my old home of Egypt in the dark.

Then we arrived in Aden, but I decided to stay onboard as it was only a short stopover. After leaving Aden the weather turned very rough and it cleared the decks of others who were stuck in their cabins, being very sick. As usual the weather didn't affect me and again, to my pleasure, I found myself alone in the bars.

Not only was the sea very rough, but it was boiling hot too, a very bad combination if you're feeling a bit green around the gills below deck. So the captain gave permission for everyone to sleep on the top deck under canvas.

'Men have to stay on one side, women on the other,' the captain barked. 'And no sneaking around.'

To be honest, sneaking around was the last thing on most people's minds. Keeping the contents of their stomach in place was more important!

I hauled my camp bed upstairs too; even though I felt fine, a cooler breeze would be most welcome. We were under a bit of cover too, so the rain didn't get to us, and straight away we all noticed how much cooler and calmer it was. I took off my uniform under the cover, folded it and put it on a bench at the end of my bed, then got under the blanket.

A few hours after drifting off, I felt a violent shaking. It wasn't the boat though, it was a furious-looking officer.

'Get up, man, get UP!' he screamed in my face.

I jumped up bleary-eyed. 'Yessir,' I cried.

'Oh!' he gasped. 'It's a woman!'

For some reason he'd spotted my uniform all neatly folded up at the bottom of my bed and presumed I was a man. He never apologised, just huffed a bit and left me to try and get back to sleep, without any success.

The next morning the calm seas had returned and we were on our way to Ceylon – what is now Sri Lanka. I couldn't wait to get off ship and explore Colombo in Ceylon. It was a real highlight of the trip.

I felt like I'd been magically transported into a different world. The women were absolutely beautiful, full of smiles, and their saris' colours were of every shade of the rainbow. They seemed perfectly in synch with the green trees, white buildings and sunshine, all a perfect backdrop. I was just absolutely staggered by it. Everywhere I looked seemed to be a postcard picture. It was such a tonic after leaving a rather grey, drab, 1950s Britain behind.

We made a trip up to Mount Lavinia as well, all of us absolutely stunned by the view, and absorbing our new surroundings like sponges. I just loved the experience. Everything was so colourful, vibrant, alive! Any worries back in Britain felt so far behind.

Before long we were back on the boat and on our last leg of the journey before we finally disembarked in Singapore. It was just as beautiful as Ceylon with an array of cultures and colours.

I was impressed by our mess too. It was large and airy and shone like a new pin. Quickly I tracked down Andy, my friend Joan's fiancé, and we had a good catch-up.

'I'll be there for your wedding, that's for sure,' I said with a grin.

'So glad you managed to get out here,' he said. 'I knew you'd do it though, Phill.'

Andy couldn't wait to give me a whistle-stop tour of the sights, so after settling in he took me straight to Bugis Street, one of the most eye-opening places in Singapore and a must-see for every tourist. Chinese music played everywhere as people from all generations, from very old folk with 'lived-in' faces to beautiful chubby-cheeked babies, were to be found sitting, standing, walking, staring at us. And it wasn't only eye-opening for me, it was taste-bud tingling too . . .

As we passed one stall after another in the bustling street, filled with the shouting and laughter of locals, I couldn't help but notice piles of green and red pods piled high everywhere.

'What are these veg?' I asked Andy as we wandered by.

'Don't ask, try one,' he said. I didn't notice the cheeky glint in his eye.

I picked one up and took a big bite. I can only say it felt like I'd just poured kerosene into my mouth and lit a match.

'Arghhhhh!' I gasped, holding my throat and spitting it out. 'Water! Water!'

Andy fell about, laughing his head off. 'It's called a chilli,' he said, offering me his flask. 'I didn't expect you to take that big a bite!'

I'd never encountered hot chillies before. The cuisine I'd grown up with was plain and predictable – all suet puddings and boiled carrots – although now I'd done a lot of travelling each new experience introduced me to something exotic.

Also rather exotic were some of the locals; we passed a few very beautiful-looking ladies, so tall and statuesque I felt like a hobbit walking past, as they looked at me.

They were so perfect, like dolls, with arched eyebrows and skin like porcelain. If it hadn't been rude, I'd have wanted to reach out and touch them, stroke them, just to see if they were real. I simply couldn't take my eyes off them.

Then Andy whispered, 'You'd never have guessed they were men, would you?'

I drew in my breath, my hand flying to my face. I'd heard of lady-boys before but had never seen one up close.

'I only wish I looked like them,' I chuckled.

My new job was as supervisor on the military exchange in Tanglin, but I soon found it very boring. There weren't very many calls and once I'd trained everyone I found myself shuffling papers and clock-watching. In fact, I was so bored I started answering calls personally to give myself something to do, but this was frowned upon.

'You're a Sergeant, not an operator anymore,' my superior sniffed at me.

Thankfully, I had my time off to look forward to, and my new social life became a reason for living. We left work at 4.30 p.m. and had tea and sandwiches in the mess, before a post-dinner rest and then a little sleep. Around 8 p.m. was when things kicked off and I'd have a bath and get ready for a night out, often staying out until the early hours.

I'd bought myself a whole suitcase full of dresses to wear for the evenings. I'd learned how many I might need in

Egypt. When I turned up in the shop in Kensington High Street and bought them all at once – lovely, colourful, classic 1950s shaped A-length dresses, all pinched in at the waist and quite beautiful to twirl in – the shop assistant serving me did a double take.

'I envy you!' she gasped. 'Wherever you're going it must be nice to be taking all these dresses at once!'

As part of my getting-ready routine, I'd usually just put on a slick of lipstick and a little blusher on my cheeks. I never painted my eyes, as I hated touching the area around them! I always had a perm done every three months and then had a wash and set once a week, so it was a case of running a comb through my hair, having a big squirt of perfume and going on my way.

We'd go out in a gang and find the nearest bar or dance to stay for the night.

I'd often be dog-tired during the day but I didn't care; I just wanted to make the most of life out there. There was so much to enjoy. The shopping centres were amazing and tailors could knock up a dress for you overnight for next to nothing. It was also a real treat to have ladies' hairdressers everywhere. They could transform your hair in a couple of hours, again very cheaply.

This was aside from all the bars, restaurants and beautiful beaches. It really was a time of fabulous fun. Often we'd visit the same hotel, where one of the girls who used to be in the army with us had a singing turn.

When my leave came up I was spoiled for choice as to where to go. But Penang was always on the top of the list, as

Winifred aged
about 5 or 6

My brother Clifford
at the same age

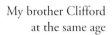

George Wheeler, the
only man I ever loved

Taken in front of our billets
in Fayid, 1949

Egypt, circa 1950

Me as a bridesmaid,
Singapore Cathedral, 1956

Me in Nicosia, Cyprus, 1958

Germany, 1960

Taking dictation for a
Colonel, 1964

Christmas party, 1964.
General Turner Cain
and his PA, me, at back

Outside quarters in
Singapore, mid-1960s

Tramps' Ball, Singapore, 1965

WRAC Sergeants' Mess, Singapore

Liphook Warrant Officers' course, 1962. Me 2nd row, 3rd from left

Reunion of Wassell Grove Workers 1941-46, held in 1983. Me at front holding bouquet

Folkestone 2007 receiving the Pingat Java medal for service in Singapore

Me with certificate for abseiling down Darby House, 1996 in Telford, in aid of Cancer Research

Meeting Prince Harry

Sharing a joke with a fellow resident

A day out in Hyde Park

Here's looking at you, Win

Mum's Army

I'd heard how unspoiled and beautiful the beaches were. So I asked my officer, who had to give me permission to go there. We were allowed to use military ships or planes if they were going that way, and luckily I was granted leave to go.

Chapter Fourteen

Rites of Passage

The journey there was an experience in itself. We had to travel by train up through Malaya, and at that time communist terrorists were battling across the country and jungle warfare was still rife, with rebel fighters trying to gain new ground. Our train was heavily guarded and we had to have a bogey in front of the engine to clear away any bombs from the track, which was in parts just a one-line system.

Once there, I had a delightful two weeks' swimming and sunbathing. We didn't wear any sun lotion in those days so usually I got a little burned and then went a very dark shade of brown.

Finally it was time for Joan's wedding and I couldn't wait. I was honoured to be her bridesmaid. Of course, everyone I talked to seemed to say to me, 'It'll be your turn next, Win,' or 'When will it be your turn?' and I'd nod and smile and say, 'Not likely . . .'

It was very much the convention, even among army ladies, to get hitched at some point or another, but for me, I just never thought about it. I was too much of a day-to-day type of person and was too busy living life to the full. I suppose I had learned early on how short life can be and not to be always fretting and worrying over my future.

I was happy to help Joan prepare for her big day though, and what a palaver it was, with all the flowers, clothes and cake to prepare. I enjoyed it in the main and loved putting together her nosegay, as there were so many beautiful and exotic flowers to choose from in Singapore.

Joan spent the last few days in her flat before getting married, which was great fun. Although I was rather looking forward to all the pomp and ceremony being over, there was such a lot to think about that we often stayed up late talking about what needed doing.

On the day of the wedding, Joan woke me up standing over my bed looking like she'd seen a ghost.

'Joan, whatever is the matter?' I cried, sitting bolt upright.

'That's it, Phill,' she said, sadly. 'I've decided I can't do it. I want to call the whole thing off . . .'

She filled up with tears and sat on the end of my bed.

I didn't say a word to her, but leaped up and went into the bathroom. I turned on the taps of the bath, put in the plug and poured some bath salts in. Then I came out and told her what to do next.

'Get in there and have a soak, Joan,' I ordered. 'You'll feel differently when you get out . . .'

I poured myself a strong drink – I can't remember what, but it wasn't a cup of tea – and gulped it down as I waited for her to get out. She couldn't pull out of it now. I just hoped she was going to come to her senses!

To my great relief, she emerged with a towel wrapped around her and wet hair, smiling. 'I'm OK now,' she said, and she never said another word about it. Although I couldn't stop pouring either of us drinks until she'd been officially declared Mrs Anderson at the beautiful ceremony in St Andrew's Cathedral. After all, as bridesmaid I suppose I felt some responsibility that she would actually go through with her big day!

The happy couple then went on their honeymoon in the Cameron Highlands. This was an area named after William Cameron, a British surveyor who was given the job of mapping out the region for the colonial government in the nineteenth century. It was a series of beautiful green hills and valleys on fertile soil where they'd built rest houses and golf courses and the like. The air was so pure and fresh up there compared to the bustling Singapore we knew. It really was the perfect honeymoon destination.

By June 1956, it was time for me to return to England. I'd completed eight years of service by now and had, on the whole, loved it. But I had a real longing now to change tack a bit and leave the signals for another job in the army. I'd grown tired of the humdrum life at the switchboard and wanted something more rigorous and a new challenge. Clerical work had always appealed to me, after a stint on the ship as a Sergeant in charge of the girls when I'd had a go.

Dad had started writing regularly and was nagging me about leaving the army altogether.

'Why don't you come and join us for a while? Get a job and settle down?' he kept pleading in letters.

He never said so, but I suspected he just wanted to try and make amends a little for our broken family. Life for him was very stable now. He'd been with Olive for years and I dare say maybe he even missed me. My brothers only came to visit him occasionally, so now he turned to me to be more involved in his life. But this was hard as I'd grown used to managing without a father. Now I was nearly thirty I felt even less of a need for him.

But Dad didn't give up and just kept up a campaign of trying to persuade me to quit.

I must admit I'd also started to imagine what life would be like on civvy street again. Once you'd joined a regiment, like I had the signals, you couldn't just swap with something else. I'd have to leave the army completely and then join up again and start from scratch. Now it preyed on my mind this was an option.

So, against my better judgement, I relented with Dad and somehow found myself handing in my notice and being demobbed. I knew I didn't want to continue in the signals. Maybe this was time for a fresh start?

I handed in my notice, much to the surprise of some of my colleagues.

'Why are you doing this, Phill?' a few asked.

'It's what suits me for now,' I told people.

I knew I'd keep in touch with many of them,

including Billie and Joan, but I had to do what was right for me.

And so I found myself meeting Dad at Coventry station platform, this time as a civilian.

'I am so glad you've come, Win,' he said, taking my suit-case.

I wasn't so sure, but I was pleased to have left the signals. I decided to get myself some work in an office to see me through before I joined up again.

But within just a few days I realised I'd made a dreadful mistake. Dad had been behaving really rather nicely to me, as was Olive . . . for the first couple of days.

Then one evening after dinner, I said to Dad, 'I'm going to go out this evening.'

I didn't know many people in Coventry, but decided to have a wander around, and see if there were any dances on.

'She's got to be back for nine-thirty if she does,' spat Olive to Dad.

I glared at her, full of absolute loathing. I was twenty-nine by now and had travelled the world, staying out until 6 a.m. sometimes. How could she try and put a curfew on me? I really wanted to say to her, 'Why, Olive? What's going to happen at nine-thirty?' The daft thing was, I probably didn't even have anywhere to go at this time, but it was just the principle of it.

I smiled tightly and decided to stay in. Dad being Dad just went along with what she said, so I knew it was time for me to move on again.

The following morning, I packed my bag and told them I was leaving to go and see Ken. But I'd no intention of coming back. I honestly couldn't get away fast enough.

As usual, my brother welcomed me with open arms.

'I don't blame you for leaving,' he chuckled when I told him about Olive. 'You did well to last a couple of days with her!'

I was grateful for his support and I talked through my decision to leave the army.

'I loved it,' I said. 'But it's the only way to swap regiments, even if it seems barmy to leave.'

Ken understood though. I just needed to get a job to see me through.

Several weeks later, I managed to find a temporary job working on the switchboard at a nearby hotel. This was my attempt at a proper job on civvy street, but it ended up rather an unpleasant experience. For a start I found it profoundly boring and, secondly, I couldn't bear many of the hotel patrons.

When one more couple wafted in with a pile of suitcases demanding this and that, I wanted to scream at them. Being polite to stuck-up snobs or rude members of the public really was hard to stomach. After a few months I left.

Even though I'd only been out of the army for a matter of months by now, I decided to re-enlist in the WRAC and this time start my career as a clerk.

I could only hope now the army thought this was as good an idea as I did!

*　　*　　*

In December 1956, I rang the WRAC office to discuss this idea.

They seemed amenable to my coming back, so I thought I'd see what I could demand beforehand.

'If I come back, can I have the rank of Sergeant back?' I asked. 'And also can I come out of signals and become a clerk and also can I get training?'

I said it in one long breath, keeping my fingers crossed at the end of the phone.

But the answer was a resounding 'yes' to all three questions and that was that. I was back in! I also spoke to a WRAC friend of mine and she persuaded me to change my combined service to twenty-two years. Originally I'd agreed to eight years, during my first stint. But if I went for twenty-two I'd be eligible for an army pension.

I was so happy to be waving my piece of paper to the training department at Guildford, knowing I didn't have to repeat my basic training, and then on to Yeovil where I got my stripes back.

It felt a bit like going back to school after the holidays. The camp was a large one and my clerical training was very thorough. There were various ranks there but we were all treated the same.

As a Sergeant I was billeted in the Sergeants' mess, which was mixed. I realised by now I preferred this, as I really got on with men better than women in many ways. I enjoyed their camaraderie; maybe it was having brothers that helped.

One evening though, one of the boys had a joke with me,

which frightened the life out of me. He was in the guard box and when I arrived back late he actually pulled his gun on me.

'Halt!' he ordered, as I approached in the dark.

It was the first time since being in the army this had happened to me, and it sent a shiver down my spine. None of us women were allowed to train with weapons and the thought of picking up a gun and using it was just something I never ever wanted to do.

Now here I was literally staring down the barrel of one.

'It's me, Phillips,' I cried.

He half-smiled, then sent me on my way. I soon suspected he was just having a joke with me, not that I saw the funny side at all.

At the end of our course we were informed of our postings and this time I was posted to Cyprus, which was then still a British colony. And this time the only way I could get there was by plane, as ships weren't used anymore. The thought of this was utterly terrifying, as I'd never flown anywhere before this point. The very thought of being thousands of feet above the ground with no way of getting out alive if anything happened just turned me to jelly. I really started worrying about it, and when it got to the point that I couldn't even drop off to sleep, I went to see my doctor.

He quickly prescribed me some sedatives and I knew I'd just have to get on with it.

We were due to take off from Southend airport at 9 a.m. and I was in charge of a few girls and some kids as well, children of some of the soldiers. This made life a bit more tricky from the beginning and, to be honest, I was more worried about getting myself through the experience than anyone else. Thankfully the children were very well behaved. I found myself downing a few beers before departure and this, coupled with the sedatives, meant I was feeling rather woozy and happy by the time take-off arrived. As far as I was concerned I was only responsible for anyone between take-off and landing, and while we were in the air I let myself drop off to sleep.

Suddenly I was shaken awake and found myself looking out of the window in wonder at the tiny airstrip below and the shanty-type roofs of the basic houses.

We'd arrived before I knew it – flying hadn't been as bad as I'd imagined it would be.

As much as I loved Singapore, I hated Cyprus with a passion. Right from the start we were greeted with suspicion and contempt. At Nicosia airport our belongings were rifled through roughly by our own boys, as it was their job.

'What are you looking for?' I asked one of the guards standing watch.

'Bombs . . . knives . . .' he snapped.

I laughed. 'As if we'd bring any in,' I said quietly. But he looked straight through me.

The atmosphere couldn't have been more different from beautiful, relaxed Singapore. Hardly surprising, I suppose, as the Turks and Cypriots were still fighting and it was a dangerous, volatile place.

Our destination was Episkopi in the southern part of the island. It was as bleak and uninviting as many of the people. The only redeeming feature was a beautiful beach.

Thank goodness, I thought. I couldn't stand the prospect of staying in such a godforsaken place without anything at all to look forward to.

The following day though, my dreams were dashed.

'We can't use the beaches,' said one girl grimly. 'They are out of bounds.'

I wanted to cry. It seemed like such a sacrilege to stop anyone even enjoying the beauty of the country. It was bad enough there was so much bloodshed and violence, but nobody could enjoy a minute's peace anywhere either.

Soon after we arrived we realised the extent of the brutality and danger. One morning a terrible racket woke up half the camp. Thick acrid plumes of smoke rose from the gateway to our barracks and people were screaming and running everywhere outside.

'What's happened?' I gasped.

'A bomb,' someone said.

Chaos ensued for a while, as police and more officers arrived to assess the damage.

A few hours later we were told an ambulance had been blown up outside our gate. Fortunately nobody was in it, but it was the Greek-Cypriots who were responsible. It was another sign of how volatile the situation was, with Greek and Turkish elements at loggerheads, and both of them fighting the British in a bid for independence.

For the most part I felt like a prisoner in Cyprus, as women were banned from leaving our cantonment between 1957 and 1959. It was just seen as too dangerous, although some of the girls working for the special operations teams were driven up to the mountains once in a while.

When I asked what they were doing, I was told they were sent to search the Greek women in the village up there for weapons. Often the menfolk would conceal them on their wives and children to try and avoid detection. I was grateful I never had to do this.

In early 1958, I was having lunch in the hotel while on a course in Nicosia, when someone came running through to see me.

'Miss Phillips, please go and see the PA to the Governor of Cyprus.'

'What, now?' I gasped.

'Yes, now,' she said.

I immediately knew something must have happened. You were only ordered to see the PA if there was news from home. And I wasn't expecting any. I felt a bit sick as I went up to her room. It could only be something bad.

I knocked, waited and was beckoned inside. Her face told me it was grim.

'Miss Phillips, I am afraid I have some bad news to inform you of,' she started.

I felt a burning flush run over my face.

'Is it one of my brothers?' I asked, calmly.

'No, it's your father,' she said. 'I am afraid he has died.'

I walked back to the hotel in a daze, my mind trying to think of what to do next.

I longed to talk to my brothers, and I wondered how Olive would cope without Dad. A thousand questions raced through my mind. But at the same time, as I always did when it came to Dad, I felt quite detached.

I went to see my superiors.

'I need to apply for compassionate leave, please, for my father,' I said.

'Is he ill?' she asked.

'No, ma'am. He has died.'

'I'm sorry to hear that,' she said, 'but also sorry to inform you, you cannot take compassionate leave if someone has already passed away. It is only for serious illnesses.'

I couldn't believe what I was hearing, but the crux of it was, I wasn't eligible for any special leave whatsoever – I'd have to use up my normal leave and I'd have to pay for my own passage home.

I didn't hesitate buying a ticket and giving up my leave though.

The journey home was spent in a daze and two days later I found myself walking up Dad's street in Coventry.

One of his neighbours, Joyce, spotted me.

She came out. 'Hello, Win,' she said. 'I'm sorry to hear your news.'

'Thank you,' I said.

I hadn't had a chance to tell anyone I was coming home

and I wanted to change into my uniform and freshen up before I arrived.

'Can I come in and sort myself out?' I asked her. So I ironed my uniform and dressed again, while Joyce told Ken I'd arrived.

Ken opened the door and, saying nothing, gave me a huge hug.

Olive heard my arrival and came to see who it was. 'How did you get here?' she gasped. 'I don't have any money to pay towards your flight, you know. I can't afford it.'

It was the sort of response I was used to from Olive, so I just looked on coolly at her.

'It's fine, Olive,' I said. 'I've already paid for my ticket myself.'

That afternoon Cliff took me to where Dad was lying in the funeral parlour. He looked the same, just pale and asleep.

I stared at him. My father. Dead. I wondered where my tears were and then decided not to worry about it. I saluted him smartly and turned heel and left. Driving home, Cliff and I sat in silence, lost in our own thoughts, but both dry-eyed.

I was so pleased to see Norman, Ken and Cliff again, along with their wives, Kath, Phyll, and Joyce. It was a treat to be with them.

The funeral was sad, but I can't say I was overwhelmed with grief. Maybe I was more saddened by what could have been than what was. The day Mum packed us on that train was the day our family had been broken for ever. Dad hadn't been capable of repairing it and, because we were just kids, neither were we. Although we'd had a rough start I marvelled at the way myself and my brothers were. Although we weren't a close family, we enjoyed each other's company and were always there for each other. Despite our parents' failings and the broken home we'd suffered, it hadn't broken any of us. In fact, I think it had made us more determined to live life to the full.

After Dad's funeral, we all gathered back at the house, where Olive was fussing with sandwiches.

We all stood around, trying to avoid her, when Norman whispered, 'Come on, let's go to the pub.'

So myself and my brothers all trooped out and toasted a drink to Dad by ourselves. As ever, we got chatting and had quite a giggle, being all together again.

Later I heard how 'disgusted' Olive had been at our behaviour. 'Their father is lying dead and all they can do is go to the pub for a drink,' she kept tutting to the wives. The reality was we just wanted to get away from her.

When I returned to pick up my case, she grabbed my arm. Her face was puffy from crying and she did look so upset, I couldn't help but feel for her.

'Are you staying?' she asked.

I paused. But I knew I couldn't.

'I'm going back with Norman,' I said gently, and left her with the neighbours.

Four weeks later I found myself back on the plane to Cyprus, feeling so low. It wasn't a nice place to go back to, but I'd done my duty for Dad and now I was back doing it for my country, and I was to be Orderly Room Sergeant, one up from Staff Sergeant. This position included making sure the orders of the officers above me were carried out to the letter, especially in the orderly room where all the admin was carried out. A new challenge.

Chapter Fifteen

The Long Game

The only way to get any respite was to go abroad on leave. And on my first opportunity I did with Pat, a lovely girl I was friendly with in the Sergeants' mess. In October 1958 we booked a trip to Tel Aviv in Israel. One of the best things about army life was all the different people I met. Friendships, as did people, came and went and we really were like one big family. There was always someone to go on holiday with, someone to chat to, someone to share your fears or hopes.

I'd never been happier to get out of the barracks and away for two weeks.

When we arrived, we bought an orange juice at a nearby café to soak up the atmosphere. Already we knew it was a much calmer, kinder place than Cyprus.

'Goodness, this juice is absolutely delicious,' Pat cried, after taking a gulp.

I tried it too and it was. I'd never ever tasted anything like it, so fresh, sweet, tangy all at once. We ended up drinking gallons of the stuff on our little trip.

Our hotel rooms were incredible compared to what we'd left behind. With air-conditioned rooms, private showers and soft beds we felt like we'd landed in the lap of luxury . . . well, in comparison to the starkness of the camp we had done.

The nights out were great fun. We found a couple of the lads from Cyprus also on leave and hung out with them for one evening, finding ourselves in a nightclub. The Israelis hadn't caught up with our favourite dance routine of the time, the jive, but that didn't stop us.

'Shall we?' I said to Pat, taking her hand.

'Let's do it!' she laughed.

And we went for it, jiggling around, moving our hands and feet in time. I could feel all eyes swivel to watch the spectacle we were making of ourselves, but I didn't care. I just wanted to have fun. And there was no better way of losing yourself than having a good jive.

Finally the tune changed and we stopped. Everyone broke into huge applause, cheering and whistling. We laughed and took a bow.

'I think we've brought jiving to Israel,' Pat giggled.

We climbed into our beds at 3 a.m., but didn't stop for long as we had an early morning call at 6 a.m. We'd booked seats on a coach tour to Haifa, passing through Caesarea, where we saw interesting excavations of this town founded by Herod the Great, then on through the Sharon Plain with its famous wine cellars before we finally reached Haifa, known as the 'Naples of Israel'. From there we went to Nazareth, in many ways the highlight of the journey.

To see the town associated with the early years of Jesus Christ was wonderful. We visited Mary's well, Joseph's workshop, the Church of the Annuciation and other holy sites. I felt so humbled to see them. I'd been a practising Catholic now for years, and to see where Christianity began was a little mind-blowing.

We went on to the Sea of Galilee, and the Tabgha site where Jesus performed the miracle of the loaves and the fishes. The next day was the Jewish sabbath and everywhere was very quiet until the evening when we decided, along with half the population it seemed, to go window shopping.

We were just listening to market traders and watching the hustle and bustle, when a man with a beard in front of us suddenly turned around.

'You following me?' he said.

'No,' I replied. 'I'd never even noticed you before.'

'Are you tourists?' he asked.

'Yes,' I replied.

We always tried to keep it to ourselves that we were enlisted.

'Do you want us to show you some night-life?' he said.

I shrugged my shoulders and looked at Pat. The man and his friend looked harmless enough, so we decided to join them. They took us to another nightclub and made us laugh all evening. One of them, called Raffir, turned out to be a top tennis player in Israel. Although he was quite a charming gentleman I wasn't at all interested, and he unfortunately took a shine to me.

'Will you come to the beach with me?' he kept slurring after a few drinks. 'I will take you away to Eilat, on the Red

Sea, look after you for the rest of your life. Make family with you. Go on,' he said, leaning in closer. I could smell the drink on his breath. 'I will show you happy days.'

I kept pushing him away, until finally I'd had enough.

'Not on your nelly!' I cried, grabbing Pat's hand. 'C'mon, Pat, let's make a move.' And somehow we escaped.

The following day we took a trip to see the Dead Sea, something that turned out to be a bit of a highlight. Firstly we ended up on a coach that stopped in the middle of nowhere – or that's what it felt like. Then our guide set off a flare and a return flare responded across the horizon. Then, as if in a film, a whole group of Arabs on camels appeared on the horizon.

We were then driven to the Bedouin camp. Here there was a large open tent where we were served with coffee. I absolutely hated their thick, black, sickly coffee, served in tiny cups, but we couldn't refuse them, as the Arabs just sank to their knees in front of us, waiting for us to drink it all up. Urgh! It was considered an insult not to drink.

Eventually we had to sit down in the tent on some cushions and wait for the meal to be served.

'I wonder what it is,' I whispered to Pat. 'I'm starving.'

But when our plates arrived, I soon lost my appetite. There on the plate lay a meal that was actually looking back at me . . . a sheep's eyeball was our main course, with rice.

'Aye, aye,' joked Pat, wiggling her plate. 'It's very different from mince and tatties, isn't it?'

We were supposed to eat with our right hands, rolling the rice into a ball and then throwing it into our mouths. I managed to sneakily throw most of my meal over my shoulder instead.

Afterwards the sheikh put on a mock court trial for us to watch and then finally it was time to go home. On the way, one of our party, a woman, jumped on a horse, which caused much shouting and hand-waving from the sheikh. It was seen as a sacrilegious thing to do. I think those poor Arabs were glad to see the back of us by the end of that day.

We weren't glad to be leaving Israel though, and I felt very sorry to be returning to our awful camp in Cyprus later.

When we touched down, it was back to the bad atmosphere, exactly the same as when we'd left. A staff car was at the airport to take us back to Episkopi. Pat and I shrank back down in the seat as it weaved its way through the bustling crowds. We had to endure all the road blocks and there seemed to be more than ever. Each time we had to get our ID papers out and be glared and stared at by soldiers.

'It's so unnerving,' I whispered to Pat after our third stop.

'Why is security so tight?' Pat asked the driver.

'Haven't you heard?' he said. 'Last Saturday, the wife of a British soldier was shot dead in the street in Famagusta while she was out shopping.'

We shuddered and shrank back further in our seats. On arrival back in camp, we were told all British females were confined to their quarters.

Despite all the dangers and general unease, we tried to make our fun wherever we could. The boys used to come down to our mess, leaving their guns at the door, as weapons weren't allowed in. Our place was seen as an area to relax, have a drink and a laugh. I always got on well with the men and one in particular I grew close to was nicknamed Gripper.

One week, some of the men were sent home and Gripper was the only one left, so we found ourselves on our own a lot and grew even closer. He asked me to go to a dance in Paphos with him. I went along, but when we arrived another lad who was soft on me was already there. He started buying me drinks and the next thing I knew Gripper disappeared in a huff.

'If that's the way you want it,' he snapped, before grabbing his coat.

I turned to the other lad and laughed; I really tried not to take any of this very seriously!

Our superiors finally decided because life was so bleak on camp a pantomime would cheer us up. Even if we'd had no acting experience or were quite shy, we weren't to have any choice in the matter.

'You, you, you and you will do it,' our quartermaster said, pointing to a few of us in the mess. And that was as far as the auditioning went!

We'd no idea how we were going to do this, but it was one way to combat the boredom so we threw ourselves into it.

It was decided we'd do *Babes in the Wood*. I ended up with three parts as there weren't enough people to go round able or willing to do it. In the end it was all rather enjoyable, rehearsing and sorting out costumes. It certainly made many an evening fly by and we all had a laugh doing it. The show was put on in Episkopi for the public and then we had to go to Paphos to entertain the Durham Light Infantry.

Part of my role was to appear onstage wearing nothing but a swimsuit. Goodness me, I had a few blushes about doing that to begin with, but I soon became a pro about it. In one scene I had to crawl along the floor like an animal and I soon found myself really going for it.

Before we performed in front of the lads, our quarter-master director gave a good piece of advice.

'Don't start speaking until everyone is quiet,' he said. 'Otherwise you'll never get a word in edgeways.'

With all the whooping and yelling when we came onstage this was so true. We waited until they showed us some respect first before we carried on. By the end of our show, men were almost falling over themselves, but we were whisked away to other quarters to take off our costumes and make-up.

In terms of boosting everyone's morale the idea of a panto was inspired and it really worked.

Afterwards we all had a drink and ended up having to sleep over in the Light Infantry tented camp, so men and women were sleeping in similar quarters, something which was never heard of before.

In the morning, I found myself sharing a water trough with a man shaving his face while I was cleaning my teeth.

'Bet this is a treat for you lads,' I joked.

'Not half,' he replied, playfully nudging me out of the way.

*　　*　　*

At New Year 1959 though, my raised spirits were soon to be defeated again. And in a way I could never have foreseen at the time.

I was working in the orderly room, filing documents and overseeing the day-to-day running of the office, when one of the girls ran in.

'Oh blimey, two of our girls are missing from the netball match. We're short!' she cried.

I'd heard about these two Privates. They'd been sunbathing on the cliffs near our barracks, when one of their towels was blown over the side. One had gone after it and slipped, falling onto a ledge, and when the other girl had gone after her, she'd slipped as well. The pair of them were in hospital recuperating.

This netball match had been the talk of the barracks for weeks. Now it was looking unlikely. Except my ears pricked up. I'd played netball all the way through school and rather fancied myself as a good shooter still.

'Can I help out?' I asked Major Metcalfe, my superior. 'I used to be a good shot back at school.'

She half-smiled. 'Well, Phillips,' she said, 'if anything happens to you too, I'll kill you, as we cannot run this place without you!'

I laughed. 'It's only netball . . . what on earth could happen?'

So it was agreed, I'd help in the team. I was positioned as either Goal Attack or Goal Shooter, and got my little shorts and top on. My plimsolls didn't fit especially well but I thought they'd do for the match. I felt a little out of shape, to be honest, as my life in the office meant far less running around than usual, but I vowed to do my best.

I was sure once I got into the swing of it, I'd be off!

It all got off to rather a good start, I really enjoyed it and got stuck right in. I had a few shots at the net, and a few near misses.

'C'mon, Win,' I told myself. 'You can do this!'

Then, halfway through, I found myself clutching the ball and aiming at the goal in a great position. Giving it my best shot, I jumped as I shot it skyward, and landed awkwardly on my left foot.

'Owwwwwwww!' I screamed, as I crumpled to the floor. The umpire's whistle blew and everyone crowded around me.

'I can't get up,' I cried, as people tried to help me to my feet.

I was in absolute agony. Despite this, one of the first thoughts that flitted through my head was: I hope I don't have any holes in my knickers! Even then I was worried about looking smart.

I was helped back to the Sergeants' mess where they cut my shoe off my foot. It had already swollen up to twice the size. It was a Friday and although I was crying in pain, I wouldn't be able to get to the hospital until Monday, as there was no transport available. Also I suspected people just thought it was a sprain.

I couldn't even hobble to the loo though, and two of the girls had to pick me up and carry me to the deep-trench latrines. It would've been funny if it wasn't so very painful and rather humiliating.

'Oh Phill, you'll be OK,' they assured me. But the size of my foot didn't. By the next day it was unrecognisable and had swollen even further.

Everyone made a fuss of me, made me food I liked and made sure I was stocked up with painkillers. Then finally Monday morning arrived and I was taken to hospital in Akrotiri. There was only a green ambulance to take me, something we called a 'meat wagon', the most uncomfortable form of transport you can imagine, as you felt every bump and jolt in it. I tried to hold my leg in the air to cushion it from all the jolts, but it didn't do much good as we bounced along rather rough terrain.

'Argh,' I groaned, as we turned the corners.

'Sorry!' yelled the driver. 'Nearly there.'

I was used to a lack of luxury on camp by now, but in this amount of pain I'd have done anything for something a bit more sedate.

As soon as I was in the hospital, I had an X-ray and this showed I'd actually broken my foot.

'No wonder it hurt,' I groaned.

The doctor wanted to admit me straight away but after my hospital experience from years previously with jaundice there was no way I was going in. I hated being bed-bound and the idea of languishing there and not being able to leave was too awful.

'You should really stay,' argued the doctor. But I refused.

'I'm not a glutton for punishment,' I said.

Mum's Army

Eventually he agreed I could leave the hospital with a plaster cast on. It was such a pain as I had to go back to the hospital every other day for X-rays or for it to be checked. But it was still preferable to staying there.

Life on crutches in the camp was about as much fun as cleaning latrines with a toothbrush. It was so hard hobbling everywhere and I could barely carry out my duties. I tried to avoid Major Metcalfe as well . . . I knew she wanted my guts for garters!

So I just slowly ambled around, trying to do what I could without getting in everyone's way.

One day, I'd had enough. The frustration got the better of me and I picked up my crutches and flung them as hard as I could at the Nissen hut wall. Those huts were made of metal and the racket as they rang out could be heard across the camp.

'What's happened?' the girls gasped, running through. They thought a bomb had gone off (they often did in Cyprus and we could hear them from afar).

'It's only me,' I assured them, sheepishly.

'Whatever did you do that for?' they asked, eyeing the crutches.

'I just want my foot back,' I sobbed.

I was due for a trip to Jerusalem in March. A petty officer's wife had asked me if I fancied going after her husband had refused to. And I was determined to make it! The doctor said it wouldn't be possible but, always one to prove people wrong, even my foot seemed to listen to me and by March I was fit to travel.

*　　*　　*

One day we had an important visitor in the form of a Major General. He came to visit us in the mess. Very often we'd have superiors and dignitaries come and descend on us suddenly. We'd be ordered to stand to attention and in they would sweep, often to only scan the room with their eyes or shake a few hands before they swept out again.

But on this occasion, he spoke to me. 'How long have you got left to serve?'

'About fifteen years,' I answered.

'What are you going to do?' he said.

'Well,' I replied. 'I'd like to do a shorthand course.' This was perfectly true, but I'd never been in a position before when someone had asked me, especially not someone as important as he was. I wanted to be a clerk full-time really. It was something that had been playing on my mind for some time.

The Major General turned to one of my superiors. 'See that she gets on it,' he ordered.

And somehow, this one conversation ensured that I did when I applied soon afterwards to start a shorthand course in Aldershot.

Chapter Sixteen

Tenuous Links

It was the summer of 1959 and the weather in Aldershot was near perfect. It was very hot, with clear blue skies every day. What a treat. It brightened up even our dull garrison, although we didn't have much time to laze in the sun. We were on duty much of the time.

I loved life in this Sergeants' mess. There was a lovely bunch here this time around and we all got on so well. I struggled with the shorthand, as it seemed like double Dutch to me, and it took me a long time to get to grips with it.

The course showed you how to write over 100 words a minute, by using a system of code-like patterns. It was very clever but tricky to master and drove me rather mad trying! But taking quick dictation for letters and the like was an essential part of the job.

Around this time, I got a message from Norman's wife. 'Win,' she wrote, 'you have to go and see Olive, she keeps asking after you.'

'I don't want to,' I replied, quite firmly. 'I'm afraid I just don't.'

But Kath pleaded with me, saying it would be the right thing to do. So against my better judgement, I thought I'd try and do the decent thing. After all, I was an adult and hopefully Olive could start treating me like one.

I took a train up to Coventry, getting off at the same platform where I'd arrived all those years earlier as a small child. Then I made my way up to Dad's old house. I still didn't see it as a home, and felt my heart sink as I approached the front door. This was my duty though. It felt like the right thing to do.

Olive greeted me like an old friend when she opened the door. I had to stop myself from flinching.

'Win,' she smiled. 'Thank you so much for coming.'

I noticed how much older she looked since losing Dad. My heart pricked with pity for her. Then she made some tea and started talking to me, finally letting me know why she wanted to see me. And it was basically to have someone to complain to.

'I miss him, Win,' she sobbed. 'I miss him so much. It's not fair. It's so hard to manage. Your father did everything for me.'

Briefly my heart went out to her, but then I could see how caught up in herself she was. She had little to no thought of me or my brothers as usual.

She burst into more sobs. 'I just miss him,' she repeated, her face crumpling.

'Olive,' I replied baldly, 'I've spent my whole life "missing" him to be quite honest.'

She looked at me, wiping her eyes as if she didn't quite understand what I meant. So I continued.

'He was my father before he ever was your husband,' I muttered quietly. I'd never dared say such a thing in the past, but this time the words had left my lips before I could stop them.

She glared at me, the old, cold Olive shining through her tears. We sat almost in stony silence as we ate dinner, and in the morning I left early. I'd finally been honest with her about how I really felt and she didn't like it one bit. I'd been dying to say that to her for years.

I never saw her again. She continued to write to me for a couple of years. But in one letter she mentioned something nice her neighbour had done for her.

'That's great,' I replied. 'I hope people do things like that for me when I'm old.'

It was scathing and I knew it. And this time, so did she. She never responded and I didn't miss her self-centred letters one bit.

I was relieved to get back to the camp. I felt like my army comrades did so much more and cared so much more than my so-called stepmother ever had done. I just wanted to close that door behind me now.

At the end of my stay in Aldershot I was presented with a cake. We never had the ingredients or the time to make anything like a cake on camp, so this was a real treat.

'Wow, how did you do it?' I asked. The white icing looked perfect.

But as the lads fell about laughing, I inspected it a little closer. The cheeky beggars had somehow made a cake out of anything but edible ingredients. The 'icing' was actually dental adhesive for false teeth, and the 'cake' was an upturned old tin hat.

'It's so clever!' I cried. I loved it. And it made the perfect send-off.

I then heard what my new posting would be and my mouth fell open at the news. I was due to be PA to a General in West Germany.

'I can't,' I blurted out to my officer in charge. 'I mean,' I corrected myself, 'I don't think my shorthand is good enough.'

'You'll go to Sennelager until it's improved then,' she said, ticking a piece of paper.

So off I went. This was definitely a posting I wouldn't have chosen, but I did need to improve and was determined to work hard and get the necessary qualifications. After the news of this new posting sank in, I felt really honoured. To have been offered a PA's position was a huge promotion and they were usually highly thought of.

We left Harwich for the Hook of Holland by boat and then completed the journey to Rheindahlen by bus. The Sergeants' mess was rather nice, but it was all-female and I didn't like this, for the same reason I didn't like Cyprus. Right from the start I overheard quite a lot of bitching and complaining. I always kept out of this. Life was too short to be mean to other women.

Then I was sent off to another part of West Germany to start my course.

West Germany at this time, in January 1960, was a

horrible place to be. It was just fifteen years after the war had finished and there were tanks and guns everywhere still.

There were no women's services at all on this camp I was staying in and this was a problem when it came to accommodation. They didn't want me being the only female in with the boys, so I was put in a very large hut by myself on the other side of the camp. I felt very isolated and alone in this place. It was so quiet inside I could almost hear myself breathe. I also felt a little scared. So I spoke to the NCO about it.

'Anything could happen to me in here,' I explained. 'If anyone broke in, who would I turn to?'

'Don't worry,' he said. 'Here's a whistle. If anything untoward does happen, just give it a strong blow.'

I stared at him. I wanted to say nobody was likely to hear the whistle either, but decided against complaining further. I tried to settle down in my bed that night, but wasn't really able to sleep deeply, always flinching at every little sound.

Then, a few weeks in, I was woken suddenly by a rat-a-tat that turned into a banging at the door. I bounced out of bed to the door.

'Who is it?' I hissed.

'It's only us, lass,' shouted some Scottish accents. I knew instantly it was a bunch of raucous Scottish troops. 'Can we come in?' They all started laughing, banging on the door again and jeering.

I picked up my whistle, but knew if I did try and blow it

nobody would ever hear the din above these lads. Their knocks and voices grew louder.

'Go away,' I cried. But that just made them laugh harder.

I looked around the room, feeling quite helpless. God knows what would happen if I let this lot in, they'd been drinking too.

I took a deep breath.

'Right, you lot,' I shouted. 'If you don't go away this instance, I will phone the military police.'

To my great relief, it worked and I heard them muttering to themselves as their footsteps and shouts grew softer.

I laughed. I had no telephone, let alone a line direct to the police.

A few days later I overheard an NCO talking about a Harry in the military police. My ears pricked up and a big smile emerged on my face. Surely Harry wasn't all the way out here! I made some enquiries and found his office at the military police building.

Boldly I walked up to his door and knocked on it.

He opened it, looking grim-faced, as serious as ever. For a split second he frowned.

'Harry!' I beamed. 'It's me, Win, the witness at your wedding to Dawn?'

Instantly he dropped his official serious 'work' demeanour and swept me up in his arms.

'Philly!' he cried. 'It's so good to see you! Come on, let's jump in the car and I'll take you to see Dawn.'

I was so happy to be reunited with the pair of them.

They were a lovely couple. Dawn had since left the WRAC and was a housewife in Germany, supporting her husband.

'You must come and stay with us every weekend you have leave,' she insisted. And so I did. I joined them for meals out, shopping trips, whatever they wanted to do, and was very happy doing it.

After I'd brushed up on my shorthand at last, I returned to Rheindahlen and was given a job with Army Legal Services. This posting was a real eye-opener and so different from anything else I'd done. The officers were all solicitors and barristers. But it was far from a heavy, depressing place to work. They all had a wicked sense of humour and loved cracking jokes.

It was needed, I suppose, because we were dealing with some really upsetting cases. There were a few murders when I was there. Usually it was soldiers who'd got drunk and ended up in fights, or tried to rob people.

Soon after, I met another fellow . . . and some of the girls made a few comments.

'Phill, you always land the real lookers,' they cried. 'How the hell do you do it?'

I'd no idea. I didn't consider myself to be beautiful really, but I suppose I knew how to speak to men and have a laugh with them.

It was around now that I bumped into Gripper again. He was also in the military police and he seemed to want to put the past behind us and asked me out for a drink again.

Although I was very fond of Gripper, deep down I never saw a future with him. We just got along very well and liked a laugh.

His uncle was from Shrewsbury, where Norman was now living, and so we found it convenient to travel back together when on leave. Norman did a double take when he saw Gripper, as he was the absolute spitting image of his uncle, who Norman knew well.

To make the journeys easier we bought an old car together, which Gripper agreed to drive. We went travelling everywhere in it. I couldn't drive so had to rely on him for sightseeing. We went into Holland, Belgium and down the Rhine. I was never much impressed with the European continent though. Having seen so many exotic parts of the world, it looked so bleak and seemed to be still suffering after the war. I felt so lucky not to be having to endure some of the conditions we saw.

Gripper and I had started arguing, over silly things really. Then one day, to make the peace he suggested something.

'I love you and want a future with you, Win,' he said. 'Can't we just get married?'

'Maybe,' I sighed. I knew I shouldn't have said this, but it was a case of anything to keep the peace at the time.

Before I knew it Gripper had booked a register office. He wasn't wasting any time! I was a bit shocked and not sure what to do.

'We'll be man and wife in a month,' he smiled. If I was to be truthful, I knew it was never going to happen. For me, when it came to marriage, my strong memory of the man I truly loved, George, sprang to mind. He was the only man I'd considered marrying and it was so hard to think of anyone else in those terms. Gripper was a lovely man, but I didn't want to be his wife. In fact, I didn't want to be anyone's wife. Except George's.

My heart felt heavy with sadness as his memory sprang to mind, so vividly, as if it were just yesterday we were walking along Morecambe beach, me holding his arm, braced against the cold chill of the sea but feeling so warm and happy inside.

I always had to blink a few times to try and bring myself back to the present moment. Sometimes I felt so alone. It was like nobody would understand how I felt about this; but then again, it wasn't something I wanted to share either.

Gripper was no George. However much this would break his heart.

As ever though, life moved on very quickly, and I was looking to where I was going to end up next.

In 1961, I discovered I was to be posted back to Cyprus. This was terrible news and I couldn't help but speak up to the officer delivering it.

'I can't do that,' I gasped. 'I really can't. I will have to leave the army if this is the case.'

She looked at me steadily. 'OK then, have your say and I'll listen,' she said.

I did so and then she nodded and went back to her notes.

Then the news came I was to be posted to Chester instead. This was so pleasing with Norman living in nearby Shrewsbury, working as a police officer.

Gripper was to stay in West Germany and he gave me a heartfelt send-off. 'I will miss you so much,' he said, holding me tightly.

I was being a coward, but felt so relieved I was leaving Germany. I knew it'd make it easier to break off our relationship. Which I did a few days later in a letter. Thankfully he took it very well. I think he must've had an inkling our wedding wasn't going to take place, as he'd made no preparations for it. He actually met and married another girl shortly afterwards. I was pleased for him but it made me even more certain I'd made the right decision. He was desperate for a wife and it could've been anybody.

By now, I was always batting off comments from people. Whenever you stepped out with a lad people always started telling you, 'You two will be getting hitched soon . . .' It was frustrating, as I knew I didn't want to. I longed to tell them to just buzz off.

A few of the lads I dated had proposed, but I just used to laugh it off. That was the only way of dealing with it. A lot of the army women were looking for husbands though, that was a big reason for some of them for joining up. It was a great place to find yourself a husband, so I don't blame some men for getting the wrong idea.

I wasn't scared of marriage, despite my parents' disastrous union. It was just a case of George, and nobody ever living up to him.

Being on my own never frightened me either. I was never on my own in the army and never on my own during my leave, thanks to my brothers. I always had people around me, to go on holidays with, to talk to. I just didn't see the point of settling down. Not when there was a whole wide world out there ready to be seen.

Chester is a pretty place with so much to see and do, like the castle and zoo, and I settled in fast. I was placed in a branch of the WRAC in the office there.

Sadly my job was less fun. The officer I had to work alongside seemed to take an instant dislike to me. I thought of her as a real moaning Minnie, always complaining and not being happy with anyone. It was very draining. So I was happy as Larry when I was swapped with another Sergeant who did actually like this woman.

I went to work in A-branch at the HQ, overlooking the river. Every day we went to lunch at the castle, as it was still in the hands of the military, apart from the crown courts. This meant I worked alongside the disciplining team, handing out court martial documents and keeping people in check. This was a fascinating job, especially seeing what made people tick, even though we were the ones doing all the ticking off.

While in Chester I bought a moped at the same time as my friend Sheila. I think we loved the idea of zipping around, feeling free and independent. But it turned out I didn't have the best hand and eye co-ordination! I was constantly falling off it and we were like two girls on a suicide mission every time we left the barracks.

The boys thought it was hilarious and always poked fun. 'You off to the chip shop?' they'd wheedle when they spotted me mounting my bike. 'Go on, Philly, go and get us some!'

For some reason I never seemed to have enough petrol and once had to push it back to camp. The lads quickly gathered as usual. One pulled out his Zippo lighter.

'Hey, I've got some fuel in this!' he laughed.

One day Sheila and I decided to have an adventure and drive our mopeds all the way to Shrewsbury to see my brother, a journey of about forty miles. We hadn't gone many miles when Sheila's silencer fell off, causing sparks to fly in the road.

I pulled up alongside her. 'Oh no!' I said, looking round. We were in the middle of the countryside with no one to help. I scooted off and found the nearest farm to see if anyone could assist us. The farmer gave us some string and we tied it up. We carried on and it began to get dark. I always drove behind Sheila, as her moped was faster than mine. She kept looking back to check I was still there as we hummed along the narrow unlit country roads. But then she started to get smaller and smaller and then disappeared. My moped had stopped! I yelled out but it was too late. It took her a few minutes to about-turn and come back for me.

My heap of junk had finally conked out and we ended up just pushing it to a petrol station. There were no mechanics but luckily a kind chap fixed it up for us and we set off again. By now we were about five hours late.

Norman's wife was frantic by the time we arrived. 'Where have you been? We were so worried!' she cried.

I wanted to kick my moped by then. 'I'm not sure whose idea it was to buy the blooming thing,' I moaned. But I knew it was mine!

Chapter Seventeen

Juggling Duties

In 1964 I was promoted to Warrant Officer Class II and was thrilled to be posted back to Singapore. My new role would be as PA to Major General Turner Cain, something that absolutely put the fear of God into me.

Major General was one the highest ranks in the army and the thought of working so closely to such a position was terrifying. There was so much responsibility and, so it seemed, room for things to go terribly wrong. But this was the job I'd landed, so I vowed to do it to the best of my ability. I'd already turned down such a position once before in West Germany.

There was an ADC between me and the General, and it was his role to deal with the General directly on some matters, while I dealt with the personnel side of things.

It was always so busy. I had to deal with everything from dinner invitations to organising cars and aeroplane tickets. The irony was that he never dictated letters, so I never needed to use my shorthand!

I soon settled into the female Sergeants' mess. I was the only woman working in the General's office, but I lived with the girls at night.

Mum's Army

It was this time around I managed to overcome my phobia of snakes. I had hated the things before, but someone showed me how to kill one instantly. You had to get a strong stick, raise it high above your head and bring it down very hard on the back of the snake's head (in the neck – if a snake has one, that is!).

Once I'd killed one, I knew I needn't fear them as much.

The girls in the quarters soon named me 'Phill the Chief Snake Killer', a title I was quite proud to have considering how fearful I used to be of the slimy things.

Every time a snake was found, someone would shout: 'Quick, call Phill!' After killing it we had to bag it up and take it to the medical centre, where they would identify the type of snake. Some were poisonous, but not many. Once though, I was in bed asleep when one of the girls shook me awake, breathlessly.

'We need you, Phill! There's a snake in the bathroom.'

Wearing my nightie, I ran inside and found a horrible-looking thing slithering along the floor. As I grabbed a stick and raised it above my head someone's hand shot out.

'Stop,' yelled one of the girls. 'That's a poisonous one.'

She went and grabbed a bucket of hot water and threw it over the snake as it rose up to strike.

'Quick!' I yelled, as we both fell backwards, trying to get out of the room.

The door of the bathroom was slammed shut as someone ran to get help from the medical staff. Indeed, it was highly poisonous and not worth the risk.

I was the only woman in the whole office but I didn't mind at all. I felt comfortable and the lads treated me as one of their own really. We had an amazing clubhouse set in a beautiful garden to relax in at night-time. Although there were civvies typing and helping run the office, it was only military allowed in there. And all ranks mixed together, which was unusual.

Soon after I started, the General was due to fly to Borneo, so I organised all the tickets and whatnot and sorted the date into his diary. But as I checked the final documents with the office, I was told something shocking.

'Has the General had his inoculations?' an officer asked.

'No,' I said.

'Well then, he can't go to Borneo,' they replied. 'He has to be vaccinated against yellow fever and hepatitis A.'

I was flabbergasted. As I'd only just started the job it was something left to the previous PA and it hadn't been done.

'What can I do?' I cried.

'You'll have to tell him he's not going,' was the reply.

Well, when you're a PA – or anyone inferior in rank – it's unheard of to start telling people what to do, even if it is in their best interests. I didn't know what to do. Then I realised it was the ADC's job anyway, so I spoke to him about it.

'Well, I'm not telling him,' he said bluntly.

I glared at him. It was so cowardly of him to leave it to me. But there was only one thing for it now, even if I was the messenger about to be shot.

Mum's Army

The General was in his office, making calls, when I knocked on the door. I was literally trembling. I'd no idea how I was going to get my words out, but I knew I had to.

'Sir,' I began, realising my chin was shaking so hard my teeth almost rattled, 'I am afraid you cannot go to Borneo.'

His face dropped as I gabbled out the next words as quickly as possible: '. . . because you haven't had your inoculations.'

He stared at me. 'Who says so?'

'The HQ,' I replied.

He dismissed me with a nod of his head and I closed the door behind me, breathing as if I'd run a race.

A few days later the General caught the flight I'd already booked and said nothing more about it. I hoped against hope he didn't pick up anything nasty, but then again, he knew the risks.

As much as I found the job nerve-wracking, we soon found an understanding between us. I worked jolly hard, always making sure everything was as organised as possible.

Sometimes I did mess up though. Once I'd not sent a response to a dinner party request, one I didn't realise was important. As soon as I realised one was actually required, I didn't hesitate to go to the General's office to confess. I decided with every mistake I made this was probably the best way forward.

I dived into his office, closing the doors quietly behind me, my head bowed.

'What is it, Miss Phillips?' he barked.

'I'm afraid, sir,' I gulped, 'I haven't replied to an important dinner invitation.'

'And why did you do that?' he said.

'Because,' I said, standing up straighter, 'I thought it was the correct thing to do at the time.'

'Very well,' he said, dismissing me with a nod of his head.

He seemed to appreciate this tactic of mine. It meant I was always honest and never had to try and cover things up. I just confessed at the first opportunity if anything went awry.

Afterwards, if anyone tried to claim I'd done something wrong, the General wouldn't hear any of it.

'My PA never does anything wrong,' he'd bark.

I did try my best, always going the extra mile when necessary, and he realised this. Once his daughter, Rosemary, was getting married and wanted to go to Thailand for her honeymoon. I went to the embassy and queued for hours for a visa for them. Then I met an official who was very polite, always bowing graciously with his hands in the prayer position, but actually he couldn't have cared less about my request and kept saying 'No' to it.

'They have to be married first,' he insisted. 'They can't have a visa beforehand.'

'But I won't give it to them beforehand,' I insisted. 'I just wanted to get it ready for them.'

He kept refusing, saying rules were rules. But I really needed him to bend them a little on this occasion . . . it was the General's daughter, after all! So I kept insisting and refusing to leave, asking to see his superior and arguing my case again and again. It was exhausting.

Finally though, they agreed I could pick it up on the Saturday on the proviso I didn't give it to the happy couple until after the wedding.

But I went to their wedding as invited and crept up behind the best man as the pews were filling up. During a quiet moment I tapped him on the shoulder and handed him the visa with a whisper. 'Just make sure you don't give it to them until they're married with the certificates to prove it!' I said.

Rosemary told me how thrilled she was afterwards and was so grateful for the trouble I'd gone to.

I took pity on her too when her husband, Captain Simon Stocker, was placed on duty in a war zone in Borneo. We used to get sacks of the General's mail to sort as well, and I'd always bring Rosemary's letters first before anyone else's and make sure she got it personally. I knew it was terribly difficult to live without him around and could imagine how worried sick she was.

However, once the General caught wind of our little arrangement.

'Philly is *my* PA, not yours,' I overheard him scold her (the General always called me Miss Phillips to my face but the more endearing term of 'Philly' to everyone else).

Once I arranged for all of the General's kit to be stowed on his flight, and then arranged for a car to pick him up. But as I waited at the airport for him very early one morning so I could see him off, there was no sign of him. I anxiously kept glancing at my watch, as the final call for his plane was announced. I rushed up to the flight attendants.

'Please can you hold the flight?' I gasped. 'The General is on his way!'

They eyed me suspiciously. By now they knew my face and what my job was. I always made myself known to try and get things to run smoothly for my boss, even if it meant being rather insistent and forthright at times.

'We can only hold it for a few minutes,' one sighed.

'Yes, right you are,' I replied. 'Thank you.'

I frantically tried calling the General's office, only to be told he wasn't there.

My brain started working on overdrive. I couldn't allow the General to miss his plane, it would seem like I wasn't doing my job properly. The hands on the clock seemed to be rotating even faster as I racked my brains, wondering what had happened. Maybe his car had run out of petrol? Maybe they'd got tied up in traffic?

Finally the flight attendants came to me with grim faces. 'We can't hold the flight for another second,' they said.

'Just five more minutes?' I asked.

Again I called the General's office, but with no luck. Ten minutes later, I found myself staring out of the lounge window as the plane, along with the General's clothes, took off without him and I started shaking.

What on earth was I going to do now? I was terrified of his response, but had no option but to return to the office and hope for the best. When I arrived back I saw another officer, and he noticed how pale I was.

'The General has been asking for you,' he said.

'Oh goodness, I think I'm for it,' I cried. The officer disappeared and then came back.

'He says you needn't be worried,' the officer explained.

I looked at him in surprise. 'But he missed his flight,' I stammered.

'Yes,' he replied. 'But I think perhaps it was his own fault.'

He didn't need to say any more. I understood. It sounded like the General had overslept!

Soon after this another Major General, Sir Antony Read, visited Singapore. Afterwards he had lots of belongings to return.

'Will you help at all, Miss Phillips?' my General asked. 'Take Sir Antony to the airport.'

'Of course,' I said.

I took all his luggage to the airport to be signed through customs. But as they inspected it they shook their heads. 'It's way, way over the limit,' they said. 'You'll have to pay for excess baggage.'

I gulped. I wasn't sure what to do now.

'Can't you make allowances for a General?' I argued.

'No, we can't,' came the reply. 'He will have to pay.'

I couldn't afford it and the General certainly wouldn't be happy to pay, I was quite sure of that. I didn't fancy the idea of explaining that he'd have to leave some of his belongings behind either. What a predicament! So once again, I found myself arguing and pleading with the airport staff. I insisted on seeing the manager, then had to raise my voice twice and explain just how important this General's position was . . . how he needed every item . . . how I was sure they could squeeze one more bag in.

It was exhausting. Finally, after a good hour of pleading with various superiors and attendants, they refused. Half an hour later the General swept in, greeting everyone courteously as he swept into the customs area.

I took him to desk and explained he had more to pay. But as they saw the General they simply said, 'No, sir, actually everything is OK, have a pleasant flight,' and waved him through. I smiled tightly, furious they didn't agree to this beforehand but glad they had now!

Although I assumed my behind-the-scenes work had gone unnoticed, the General sent me a lovely 'Thank you' card, something he didn't have to do.

While I was stationed in Singapore there was lots of unrest, with riots between Malay and Chinese groups taking place frequently, with many arrests, deaths and injuries. The jury was out as to why these riots were taking place but some people blamed infighting between the communists and other groups, although we British had little to do with it. Often I would wake to hear bombs going off at night and occasionally we heard them during the day.

During one of the local festivals, something triggered off bad feeling among the tribes and a huge violent clash took place. We were confined to our camp for a week and were kept out of it.

In our compound, especially while visiting the General's smart house in the lush gardens, it all seemed like a world away.

Of course, it wasn't long before my next travelling experience. I just had such a thirst for it and was always on the lookout for more trips. There's nothing like getting on a boat and not knowing what you'll experience the moment you step off it.

My next destination was to be Thailand. I went with a fellow Warrant Officer, Frieda, and we booked a passage on the *Kota Kinabalu*, a cargo boat.

The weather wasn't very kind on the way there, and once again I faced the rolling seas and stormy skies of the South China Sea. It tipped it down with rain as well. Once again my tummy stayed intact, and I watched with pity as those around me ran around, looking green and retching over the bows.

Finally we reached the Gulf of Siam and sailed into Bangkok. To begin with we used the boat as a hotel, deciding to kip on it and go ashore during the day, while cargo was being offloaded.

I really fell in love with Thailand. It has something of everything: mountains, lakes, rivers, beautiful sandy beaches, and the most astonishingly lush vegetation wherever you looked. On one boat ride, I sat in amazement as rice paddies, towering clumps of bamboo, orchids of every variety and flowering trees I'd never seen before of every colour, red, yellow and purple, all rushed past my eyes in a rainbow blur. I realised then the Thais are probably one of the happiest and most contented communities in Asia, maybe because poverty is rare and they can live with plenty to eat from their own lands.

'It's love at first sight,' I cried to Frieda.

I loved the way the Thai people trained elephants to help them with the excavations of the forest lands, and then was equally thrilled to spot wild herds too.

Everywhere we went we were waved to or smiled at. Frieda was terribly attractive with her platinum blonde hair. But neither of us were interested in men at that time. We just wanted to have fun.

Our next trip was to the floating markets of Bangkok, a real spectacle worth seeing! The city was sometimes known as the 'Venice of the East' thanks to its maze of 'klongs' (canals) crisscrossing the city and the countryside. We booked a tour on a boat and found ourselves navigating a rather narrow gangway.

'Be careful,' said Frieda, as I stepped on.

I confidently walked down, but suddenly slipped.

'Argh!' I cried, falling halfway down the side. I gashed my leg all the way down and it started bleeding, dripping down my ankle.

'How elegant,' I said, managing to laugh.

I hobbled on board, tying a handkerchief around my leg. Trust me! I thought, wincing.

A few minutes later an enormous American lady started to navigate her way across.

'I bet she'll come a cropper,' I whispered to Frieda.

But she skipped on board as lightly as a ballet dancer,

making me feel even worse. I weighed eight stone nothing but could be as clumsy as they come.

Soon my mind was taken off my latest injury, as we set sail down the Chao Phraya River, seeing hundreds of early-morning market boats on the way to Bangkok, filled to breaking point with fruit and veg. We stopped at a jetty and got off to view the amazing arrays of silks being woven in a floating factory.

Later on we enjoyed a trip to the Temple of Dawn, an incredible building encrusted with shells and broken pieces of pottery and porcelain. Visitors could climb up to the spire, but I decided to give it a miss.

'I daren't risk another fall today,' I laughed to Frieda.

Then we went to the Grand Palace to see the Temple of the Emerald Buddha. I also noted how the Thais dressed up their Buddha in costume to suit the season; if it was cold they'd wear a little mac. It was a world away from the Catholicism I'd been brought up in.

No trip to Bangkok is complete without a visit to the Reclining Buddha.

Absolutely huge, at 150 feet long, we just couldn't believe our eyes. The insoles of the feet were inlaid with mother-of-pearl.

'You'd never get this in Coventry,' I smiled.

I learned how every Thai home has a spirit house (they looked a little like a bird house to me) in which the 'lord of the land or place' lives, and it usually faces the most important room of the house. Offerings are made to spirits each day, things like fruit, candles, incense, flowers or sweets.

Three days later, the captain of the cargo ship announced to us that he was moving on. This was the downside of catching a ride on these ships, you never had a say in when you came or left. But it was worth every second we'd had, and we were grateful to be hitching a ride.

On the way back we stopped at Songkhla, where while docking we hit a 'sand barrier', meaning it was a very bumpy ride. One of the girls started screaming, thinking the boat would capsize, but myself and Frieda soon explained what was happening (seasoned travellers, we were!).

When we arrived we went down to the beach. One of our group was an army officer and, behaving like the perfect gentleman, he moved a few yards away while we all pulled on our swimming costumes.

As soon as I pulled one arm from my dress though, a local man appeared, leering over a sand-dune.

'Get lost!' shouted one of the girls.

The officer heard the commotion.

'C'mon over here, fella,' he yelled.

We got changed all the more quickly after that.

The waves were so huge we didn't dare set foot in the ocean so we lazed on the sand and drank cold beer. Then we popped into a local hotel for a quick meal, probably looking like a bunch of gypsies by now.

In high spirits after the beer, we all started singing, 'I dreamed I was in Songkhla in my Maidenform', a song from an advert selling bras! I expect the locals were quite relieved when we cleared off back to the ship.

Approaching the boat was quite frightening, as the water

had grown very choppy, with another storm brewing. I clung to the sides like a child, just wanting to get on safely. As I clambered on, helped by the captain, I couldn't help myself.

'Quick, open the bar, please!' I cried. 'We're all suffering from cold and shock,' I added cheekily.

We had another fun evening, laughing and drinking beer, and by the time my head hit the pillow I was out for the count. The following morning my head throbbed, but I was soon refreshed by sitting on the deck, drinking endless cups of delicious black coffee as we made our slow way home.

Chapter Eighteen

Times A-Changing

By now Joan and Andy had moved to Kuala Lumpur, so I often popped over to see them. They loved living in Malaysia, and I loved exploring the city. The climate was very hot, with the most beautiful flowers growing everywhere, wafting their delicate scent wherever you went. Kuala Lumpur was a busy city, growing in size every year but still keeping its old buildings intact. The old government offices in the centre were built on Moorish lines and when floodlit looked incredible.

In 1965, Joan adopted a little baby boy from England and brought him home. I was so pleased for them, I was sure they'd make fantastic parents.

I went to the christening and one of Andy's friends there, a British businessman, had actually married a Thai princess. She was beautiful and a real head-turner. While she took pictures of the christening Joan joked as she knelt down beside the baby.

'Ooh, you'll never have a princess at your feet again,' she laughed.

During this time I volunteered to become the President of the Mess Committee. This meant I helped book bands and decorate the rooms for parties; it was so much fun. Once we got a jazz band in, and I made a huge papier-mâché 'decoration' to go around the area where they sat to look like a rock face. I thought it was in keeping with the room and the other decorations of palm trees.

Although we were thousands of miles away we tried to keep up with the news back at home. I was amazed to hear about all the changes and how this decade was dubbed 'the Swinging Sixties'. We felt like we existed in our own micro-cosm, separate from the rest of life back home, but occasionally news filtered down.

In October 1965 we heard how the Beatles, the most successful of all the new bands, had been awarded the MBE – presented by the Queen, no less. One evening, driving back from somewhere, I was in the front of the car with the General in the back when I turned round to tell him.

'Have you heard, sir, the mop-tops have been given the MBE?' I laughed.

He frowned. 'Well I never,' he said sternly. 'What has the world come to? I bet Rosemary will be pleased though.'

I knew so much of it was passing us by but I didn't mind. When I saw the fashion for miniskirts and loud clothing I didn't think it would suit me anyway.

One weekend I decided to take a trip to Malacca with Frieda. We left during a proper tropical downpour, which soaked us to our underwear within seconds. We shivered with cold for the rest of the journey. For part of it we took a ferry. Although we think of a 'ferry' as a boat, this was no more than a giant raft pulled by a chain. When our bus drove onboard, I held my breath, my heart in my mouth.

'I hope we make it across,' I whispered to Frieda.

Thankfully we did, but how it worked and stayed afloat I'll never know.

On arrival we went to our guest house. We shared a very large room with mosquito nets overhead. Luckily for me, they didn't seem to like the taste of me, which was just as well as we only had nets to protect us. There was no lotion in those days.

As we turned up we soon realised we'd picked a bad weekend to stay, as there was a political rally being held nearby. People were shouting and screaming everywhere and it all felt rather intimidating.

We decided to go to bed early and, as I was trying to get to sleep, I heard my friend snoring softly. It grew louder and louder, until I had no choice but to go and shake her a bit to stop the rattling and grunting! Finally I dropped off and this time woke to 'feel' something was very wrong.

I sensed an intruder, and was scared out of my wits. I couldn't hear anything, but just knew someone was standing over me.

Before I could decide what to do a huge shrieking sound came from my mouth.

'Wh-what?' cried Frieda, sitting bolt upright.

I was half out of bed as I turned to see a man running from our room. I carried on my racket, realising it was scaring him witless.

Quickly we realised we'd not locked either of the doors in the bathroom, so we did so and then tried to go back to sleep. I was so glad I'd woken when I did.

'They call this a rest house,' I said. 'But it's nothing of the sort, really, is it?'

The next day was less eventful and peaceful as we enjoyed the harbour at the mouth of the river with its seaside park, the ancient cannons on the side and the view from St Paul's Hill. It had a lovely Portuguese flavour, a hangover from the days of occupation hundreds of years earlier.

Back in the camp, I continued with my daily duties of keeping everything running as smoothly as possible for the General. He worked at the top of the house and I worked in the office below. Every time he wanted something he'd call on the telephone. I was up and down those stairs like a yo-yo.

'Can you get me some more cigars, please, Miss Phillips?' he said one afternoon.

'Certainly, sir,' I replied.

Off I went to the kiosk in the grounds of our HQ. As usual it was a lovely day and it was an errand I quite liked really.

As I arrived, a couple of the lads were deep in conversation, waiting for their turn to be served; they said hello and carried on chatting. Then a huge buzzing sound filled my ears.

Instantly I recognised it to be a boring beetle, a nasty little bug about the size of a bumble-bee, which could burrow under your skin. Usually it went for wood and so thought our compound lovely with all its tasty wooden huts.

But this one flew directly into my khaki drill dress, my standard uniform.

'Ewww,' I screamed, as I sensed it buzzing around my bra.

Overwhelmed with panic, I started screaming like a banshee, tearing at my dress. I started unbuttoning it as the buzz grew louder and I could feel it starting to 'burrow' into me.

'Get it out!' I screamed, pulling off my dress.

I sensed the two men in the queue gazing at me with open mouths, as I started to try and get my dress off, twisting and turning like a mad thing. Finally the nasty bug flew off as I sank to my knees, gasping for breath. That's when I looked up and realised I was half-undressed, with two men staring at me.

They must think I'm a sex maniac or something, I thought to myself.

Suddenly feeling quite embarrassed, I buttoned myself up and went to the medical centre. I could feel a hole in my chest and it was bleeding.

As I recounted the story to the nurse she started giggling.

'And then I ended up on my knees with my dress half off,' I explained.

She burst out laughing.

'It's all right for you,' I said, 'but the beetle did actually get to me, and I need help, thanks!'

She straightened her face. 'Sorry, it was just so unfortunate it all happened in front of a couple of fellas too.'

I had to laugh too then.

Later on I returned to the office, all bandaged up. By now the General had got his cigars from someone else and had already heard all about the story. For weeks afterwards whenever any of the boys saw me walking down the corridor they'd start humming 'The Flight of the Bumble-Bee', the cheeky so-and-sos!

A few days later the commanding officer of our unit sent for me.

'Miss Phillips, it's about time you had a change of air,' he said. 'I want you to go to the Cameron Highlands.'

This was a camp up in the hills where the air was cool and humidity didn't exist. It was normal after twelve months in Singapore that you got sent up there to enjoy the air and get some relief. I'd heard all about how beautiful it was from Joan when she went there on honeymoon. Now it was finally my chance to find out too.

I knew I'd not be able to go for long as the General was going to Penang for a few days. But after a few enquiries I was ordered to go up there anyway.

So I found myself in a vehicle on the very bendy roads to Tanah Rata, at the top. Once again I watched with sympathy as others around me were sick as dogs, having to stop on the side of the road to throw up in the bushes. I felt so lucky not to have to endure it!

As I gazed out of the window, I could see deep into the forests. It really was a world I'd never seen before, so desolate and undiscovered. At one point, I looked outside and spotted natives wearing very little, holding bows and arrows. For several seconds, I blinked hard, quite unable to believe my eyes. These were real tribesmen, living lives so differently from ours.

As our vehicle carried on they disappeared and I sat actually wondering whether I'd imagined the whole thing.

During my stay I stopped at the British military hospital up there as there were no spaces for short-stay guests at the 'change of air' station. I spent my days enjoying the scenery with long walks and relishing the beauty. There was over 3,500 hectares of forest, jungle trails and dramatic waterfalls. There were plenty of native villagers too, all jungle dwellers. Although to our Western eyes they appeared quite backward, they'd spent generations living off the land and leading peaceful, productive lives.

I was so happy to be there; even just a short walk with lizards at my feet and colourful birds flying overhead was nothing but a treat to my senses.

One morning though, I was greeted with panic-stricken faces.

'You'll never guess what,' someone said. 'You missed the tiger last night!'

Apparently a tiger with an appetite for the local dogs prowled the forest area near the mess and his spoor marks showed he'd been walking between the hospital and the mess.

'Good job too,' I laughed.

Afterwards, when I talked to someone back in the office about the natives I'd seen, they nodded.

'A few years back an officer got out of the bus on a toilet break and went to explore that area a bit,' he said. 'And he disappeared. Never seen again, and a search party found nothing.'

I returned home absolutely rejuvenated. I felt so fortunate once again to be viewing such jewels in the world.

Obviously I was doing as much visiting as possible while in Singapore, but one place, Hong Kong, was seen as the most lively, exciting, vibrant country you could visit and a 'must see' on every WRAC's list while posted in the region.

Time and again I heard the others raving about it in the mess.

'It's just out of this world!' people said. 'The food, the lights, the shopping . . .'

'It's a once-in-a-lifetime experience,' said someone else.

Yes, Hong Kong appeared to be a case of New York, London and every other incredible capital all wrapped up in one!

I continued working for a few months and then booked more leave as soon as I could. It was time for me to see this Mecca for myself!

I tried to sort out transport, but no army planes were available so I had to get a civvy one, which felt bizarre after travelling military-style usually. The first flight I tried to take was cancelled due to a typhoon whipping up the country, so I returned to camp, rather annoyed.

Eventually I got on a flight, but as we approached Hong Kong my introduction to it wasn't good. Heavy cloud hung low and turbulence sent us bouncing everywhere. Once the landing strip at Kai Tak came into view, it looked like nothing except a thin strip of tarmac built into the sea. I pressed my face against the window as I spotted a plane's tail sticking out of the sea! Obviously not all aircraft were able to hit their target!

I'd booked into a hotel for my first visit, but as my flight was cancelled, I now found myself with nowhere to go. So I called on the WRAC unit and they agreed to let me stay in the Sergeants' mess.

The girls there were all very kind and keen to show me around Hong Kong and Kowloon. Although so many people raved about the place, I couldn't see what the fuss was about. To me it was like a second-rate Singapore, and the noise drove me insane.

The deafening sound of constant beeping traffic, tinny music and bustle was overwhelming. I also found the poverty-stricken areas with their shanty huts and desperate-looking children very upsetting. There were plenty of shops, and the city was lit up like a Christmas tree at night, but I couldn't say I was impressed.

The first day, I woke early and went for a walk around the centre to try and soak up the atmosphere everyone had talked about. But it just seemed too much for me: honking cars, people shouting their wares, shops, shops and more shops. I felt like I needed to find a quiet spot for a coffee after just half an hour.

Not for the first time I wondered if, at heart, I'm not much of a city girl really.

To my mind Hong Kong was all bright lights but with no substance. The only peace I got was when I hired a car and went over to the New Territories up to the border with China. The Peak, being the highest point on the island, was also another breathtaking view, overlooking everywhere.

One highlight while I was there was a firework display. It was held every year by the Chinese, but we could enjoy from over the border. As we watched the explosions and stared in amazement at the colours, it seemed like something from a film.

For my journey back to Singapore, I called the 'movements' department to arrange an army flight home.

'Well, Miss Phillips, I think you can probably book your own. I'm sure you can afford it,' came the very curt reply.

I was quite shocked, as we were entitled to military flights if they were available, just catching them as and when they came.

So I called back a bit later and told them I worked for the General and could they see what they could do.

A few minutes later, I had my seat home.

When I got back everyone was very busy preparing for an important visit. The Duke of Edinburgh was coming to see us.

It was a big occasion and a big morale boost. We were so far from home and to be visited by a senior member of the royal family was exciting. I had to make sure everything was running smoothly for the General to greet him and it took quite a few extra hours of work.

On the day of the visit the General was keen for me to join in. 'You coming down, Miss Phillips?' he asked.

I shook my head. 'I'm sure there will be duties in the office, sir,' I said.

I was glad he didn't press me as, being honest, I always found any visits like this difficult. I knew I'd well up seeing Prince Philip too.

I'm not sure why this was. Maybe it made me feel home-sick deep down, or triggered some memory inside of me. Who knows? But it was uncomfortable for me, and I wanted to try and keep out of it.

Instead I watched all the pomp and ceremony from upstairs, where I took some great photos. In fact I proba-bly ended up with a better view than those shaking his hand.

We also had to prepare some paperwork for the Prince of Wales's upcoming investiture at the time, and my General was in charge of overseeing its smooth running, as top secret as it was. Again, this made me feel a lump in my throat. He seemed so young, so innocent, I wondered how he'd cope. I also always sort of feared the worse for these dignitaries. I've no idea where these thoughts came from, but maybe it was because I'd seen the sad side of life a few times and knew how such an event could affect the country.

The Duke's visit was a huge success and it was good timing, as things had been even trickier in terms of recent bombings. Often we'd been woken up by the distant explosions. I was never frightened, as I knew we weren't a target, but by the same token, we didn't get much sleep. Every time one went off we'd always glance at the clock, then the next day listen to the wireless reporting the bombs. And the news announcer almost always got the timing wrong on the news.

'It was two o'clock!' we'd all chorus, if they claimed it was at 4 a.m., for instance. That became a running joke.

After two years in Singapore, I was sad to know my time was coming to an end.

One day the General invited me to his house for luncheon in his garden. As ever, it was lovely to spend time with him. I'd really got to know and care for him and his family.

'Have you tried this before?' he asked, holding up an unusual-looking half-cut fruit, with a strange glistening seeded texture inside.

'No. What is it?' I asked.

'Passion fruit,' he grinned.

I took a few spoonfuls and my face lit up.

'Mmm. That is amazing,' I gasped.

We chatted about his family and general gossip about the camp, when he suddenly looked serious.

'Where would you like to be posted to next?' he asked me, as his domestic served up a boiled ham salad.

'I think I'd like to go back to Chester,' I said.

I hadn't planned to blurt this out so fast, but he'd asked the question and I hadn't expected that either!

He looked momentarily taken aback. I knew he loved having me as his PA. He often said he didn't know what he'd do without me.

'OK, Philly,' he said, quietly.

I had made this decision partly because you're advised not to spend more than two years abroad as a woman (it was three years for a man) but also it had all been such a success, I suppose part of me wanted to leave on a high.

'I think it's for the best, although I've enjoyed this very much,' I sighed.

'Very well,' he said, looking rather surprised. I could've stayed with him while he finished his tour, as it was drawing to an end soon too, but I also longed to go my own way.

Chapter Nineteen

Toing and Froing

The journey home was terrible. After a few drinks to set me up for the flight, I found myself enduring a very rough journey. As we were buffeted about I pulled a blanket up to my chin and just hoped for the best – I must have dropped off to sleep somehow, then suddenly the lights came on and I woke with a start. Then we hit an air pocket, and literally dropped downwards two miles within seconds. The sensation was terrifying as my tummy was left somewhere above my head!

I was so pleased when we finally landed and got off at RAF Gan in the Indian Ocean for refuelling and an overnight stop.

Milling around the airport in our civvies I was amused to see I was the only woman among so many men again. Then suddenly a message boomed over the Tannoy.

'Can Warrant Officer Phillips please come to reception,' it said.

I arrived to find three RAF officers laughing. 'We just wanted to check your sex,' they admitted. 'We'd heard a woman was travelling but didn't know who it was.'

'Well, thank you,' I joked back.

'We'll have to get you to sleep with the wives and children now, then,' one quipped.

'Thank you again,' I said politely. 'And there was me thinking I'd get to sleep with the fellas!'

Not that I got much sleep that night. We stayed in a hut with a tin roof and the noise of the tropical storm outside was horrendous.

Coming home made me shiver to my core as I left the Singapore sunshine behind. This time my destination was Mill Hill, a suburban part of North London and such a far cry from the exotic sun.

I didn't want to go back to London. I'd enjoyed Knightsbridge but, compared to all the other places I'd been, it felt too big and grey for my liking now. I was given a temporary post in a Stanmore office. The work was dull as dishwater, but I hoped to get something more interesting soon.

One day while I was sat at my desk, I heard a familiar voice.

'Good morning!'

I spun around to see Major General Turner Cain standing over me, beaming.

'Good morning, sir,' I gasped, standing to attention.

We had a brief chat and I felt rather sad, as I realised how much he missed me.

'You were a very good PA,' he said, wistfully.

Afterwards it turned out he'd come to see me especially. This was quite a shock for the others in the office. A General visiting always caused a stir but to think he came just to see me was overwhelming.

To relieve myself of the boredom I bought myself a car when someone mentioned they were selling one. It was a Mini, and I fell in love with it on sight.

It was so shiny and cool, not that I've ever been one to keep up with fashion. All the '60s clothes and music had passed me by really.

Now I just had the minor problem of learning to drive.

After a few lessons I took my test but failed on something terribly minor. As I went to turn right I'd apparently not moved 'far enough' into the middle of the road, according to the examiner. How frustrating!

Very quickly I realised I'd made a bad decision to return to the UK. The clerical positions were few and far between. I stuck it for a couple of months, when I just knew I couldn't take it any longer.

Then, just as I was on the point of giving up hope, a posting came up to Chester and I was absolutely astonished to find out who I'd be working for. It was General Sir Antony Read, who'd sent me that thank-you note for sorting out the airport problems.

Wow, I thought. He remembers me!

Now he was stationed in Chester, the General Officer in charge of Western Command, and I had been picked to be his PA. I was pretty thrilled to be going back there and escaping London again.

I also passed my driving test soon afterwards. Now I had real freedom in travelling and I loved touring around North Wales and Cheshire, enjoying the scenery.

Around this time, I joined the military pilgrimage to Lourdes, an incredible experience. Troops from all over the world attended and what a sight to behold it was. As we approached the religious site we could see everyone in their full uniform, with such an array of colours.

One evening we had a torchlit service out of doors, after sunset; again, such a feeling of togetherness and belonging came about.

Then on the Sunday all the sick and injured were paraded by the grotto for a blessing. Many were bedridden and disabled, praying for a miracle. It was such a moving sight.

During the trip I decided to 'go through the waters'. As usual I was always up for the experience if anything new came about. And this is something I'd definitely never done before.

I was stripped of my clothes and had to put a white wet robe on, then two attendants immersed me in the cold, fast-flowing water. It was bloody freezing and a shock to the system. I didn't feel anything different after it, but at least I'd given it a go.

After only a few months though, we were informed that Western Command at Chester was to be run down and phased out. Redundancies were being offered. I thought about this and, fearing I'd end up back in London doing a menial job, I decided to apply for it, but they turned me down.

* * *

In 1968, I was having a chat with my brother Cliff and he suddenly asked, 'Do you know where your mother is?'

I laughed. 'She's your mother as well as mine, Cliff.'

'I know,' he sighed. 'Shall we try and find her?'

'Maybe we could find out what's happened to her at least,' I said.

I wasn't sure if I wanted her to know we were looking. But I suppose out of curiosity I wanted to see what had become of her.

In the end I wrote to a missing persons charity advertised in a local paper. 'Please do not pass on my address to her if you find her,' I wrote. 'Just pass on her details to me, so her children can decide whether to get in touch.'

Sadly, they didn't listen to this and just a few weeks later I received an excited letter from Mum. I was furious. Aside from the fact that as a Warrant Officer and Sergeant Major I was used to having people listen to my requests – in this case not to pass on my details – I also felt rather uncomfortable hearing from her without warning.

She was living in Southport now and working as a house-keeper.

'I would be very happy to see you again, Win,' she'd written.

I sighed. I didn't know what to think. I was quite surprised she was so keen to meet, and I suppose curiosity got the better of me, so I agreed to, although my brothers said they weren't interested.

Looking back, what I did was actually quite generous. I booked a week away in Wales with just me and my mother to try to make up for lost time.

Meeting her at the train station, I was struck by how little she'd aged. She was still a fine-looking woman and smiled broadly when she saw me. We didn't hug; I flinched a little when I thought she'd try.

'Hello, Mum,' I said, the words sounding thick and awkward as they emerged from my lips.

'It's been a long time,' she said, as though she'd been away on holiday.

I didn't know what I was expecting but we walked to my car and I drove her to a B&B I'd booked as we made polite small talk. There seemed to be no sense of shame or regret or even any real connection on either side. We were like two strangers, spending our days walking, admiring the scenery, going for lots of cream teas and just talking chit-chat.

Nothing was said about what she did. Nothing was asked about my brothers or my life or my job in the army. I'd always felt on some level Mum had liked my brothers more than me. Maybe it was a sense of gentleness and understanding she seemed to have towards them I'd picked up on when I was little. She didn't mention Dad once and I assumed she couldn't have cared less about him either.

We were just two ladies who happened to be related, making the best of a week away. At the end of the visit, she politely thanked me for the trip, as if I were a tour guide, and we shook hands as if completing a business trip. As we said goodbye, I found myself letting out a long sigh of relief.

I knew then I'd let go of her or any hope of a decent relationship a long time ago. Both myself and all my brothers had made our own lives for ourselves. And, it appeared, Mum seemed to be doing OK on her own, too. And that really was the end of it.

Afterwards she wrote to thank me, and I think I wrote a few more times, but it fizzled out. It was a relationship apparently neither of us was particularly interested in anymore. None of my brothers enquired about the trip or how she was. We weren't a family to look into the psychology of situations or sit and brood. It didn't seem worth it somehow. The ties had been broken and in my eyes it was the doing of our parents. When they split up they really should have sat down and worked out exactly how they were going to care for the four kids they had. But they didn't. And the end result was this.

Anyway, I had new pastures to think about and was to be stationed in Whitehall, a dream job for some, but not for me. It meant pushing papers around a desk all day long with very little to do.

It was my job to oversee an office, but really we had too many hands on deck. After handing out the post and making sure the admin was done, the day dragged endlessly, but I had to make myself look busy. Many of the officers would drag out the smallest task to last all day too. It was maddening.

We had some strange requests at times. The Queen would emerge from a building near ours into Horse Guards Parade on her official birthday for Trooping the Colour.

'You have to keep a drawer full,' I was told.

'What with?' I asked.

'A comb, powder and lipstick for Her Majesty just in case of any last-minute touch-ups,' he said.

I smiled. Of course, the Queen was as human as the rest of us, but I couldn't imagine having to run across the road with a pink lipstick in my hand for those 'just in case' moments! Nowadays when I watch the Queen on television I wonder if anyone has ever had to make that mad dash!

Finally, I plucked up the courage to ask for a transfer again, but I was made to feel very guilty. Then one day I couldn't take it any longer. I went to see the bosses and told them. 'I want to get out of here,' I begged. 'Please.'

'Sorry,' they said. 'You can't.'

But this time, I was determined. I was a Warrant Officer I by now and this was the position this post was for. I had plans on what to do next if they'd said no.

'OK,' I said firmly. 'In that case I will demote myself to Warrant Officer II and you'll have to find someone else.'

They stared at me open-mouthed. How could I dare say this? I'm not sure myself, but I just knew I couldn't continue with this 'job' anymore.

Incredibly my request for demotion was approved and I applied for another posting overseas. And I was absolutely thrilled when I learned I was going back to Singapore.

It was now 1969 and I was back working as a chief clerk, one of my favourite jobs. I was determined to make the most of it, as just two years later my twenty-two years' service would be up, and I knew the chances were I'd be back in civvy street. Overseas postings were on the decline now the war was far behind us and, as I'd learned in London, there were few jobs of any interest back home.

But within twenty-four hours of arriving, despite loving the heat and the beauty of the place, I wondered what on earth I'd done.

There was very little to do in the office aside from shuffling papers! Of course, we had to look busy at all times, and this was no mean feat to carry out for eight hours at a time.

Luckily that job soon came to an end and I was back working for top brass, this time the Brigadier, who was in charge of administration for the whole of the Far East.

He was a lovely chap, very distinguished-looking (as they all were) and cool as a cucumber. The Duchess of Kent was his cousin. Her husband, the Duke of Kent, was killed in 1942 on a 'special mission' with the RAF. He was described by Churchill as a 'gallant and handsome prince' and by the looks of his pictures that's exactly what he was. I couldn't help but feel sorry for the Duchess. We met a few times. She was always so immaculate, calm, peaceful and friendly. She was genuinely interested in our work. I could see how much she admired the military.

In our office there was only me, the chief clerk, the Major and the Brigadier. The Brigadier was now doing the same job as General Turner Cain had the last time I was in Singapore, as his own workload had reduced thanks to the shrinking size of the army and the number of troops to be administered. However, with just four of us, we had plenty to keep us busy.

* * *

For my first leave on this posting, I planned something different.

After the war, my Auntie Annie's son, George, had emigrated to New Zealand. Like me, he'd got the travel bug after serving in the RAF, so he jumped at the chance of a job working for the post office in New Zealand and I didn't blame him. From pictures I'd seen, it looked so beautiful, lush and green, with so much space. We regularly wrote to each other, as I still did to all my brothers and cousins, and he asked me to go and see him.

'That shouldn't be a problem,' I replied. 'I'll try and get passage on the next RAF plane going over!'

George was so excited and sent me a catalogue of the best pictures of New Zealand. I spent every evening in bed, poring over them. I couldn't wait to go. I arranged my leave and wrote to him again to tell him when to expect me. I had booked a seat on a military plane to leave a couple of weeks later.

But a week before I was due to take off, an officer came to see me.

'Phill, we've been told there is a toilet issue on the flight you're supposed to be on,' he said.

'What's the problem?' I asked, not liking the look on his face.

'Well, the only toilet they have is a tin can on the bulk-head for the lads to use and you'll be the only woman on board,' he continued.

I laughed. 'Well, that's not a problem for me,' I said.

'It is for the flight officials. They say they can't take a female in such circumstances . . . I am sorry.'

Now it was my turn for my face to drop. I couldn't believe my passage was being stopped for the sake of me having to pee in a tin can. It seemed like such a petty rule. But I suppose they wanted to protect my dignity, even though I was sure it wouldn't bother me in the slightest and everyone could just avert their gaze!

I nodded. Rules were rules and, as I'd realised a long time ago, you just had to accept them.

'Very well,' I said.

That evening I sat down and wrote George another letter. My chance for making it to New Zealand had been dashed. Sadly it never was to be and I never saw George again.

I'd already booked my leave though and I was determined not to waste it. So I went to the steamship offices in Singapore and asked them, 'What have you got and where is it going?'

The cargo boat, the *Kota Kinabalu*, the same one I'd travelled on to Bangkok, was setting sail shortly around Borneo. So without hesitation I booked a trip. This time I was sailing completely on my own and had no idea where I was going, but that made it more exciting!

As usual, I settled into a small berth but soon went onto the main deck; I was too excited about what was coming up next. I watched as the cargo of rice and rubber was loaded and then by evening off we went, hitting the open sea for another adventure.

In the morning, I woke up to find the sun streaming through my porthole. I went out on deck to find it completely deserted, so I chose the best spot in the sun and set up a chair to soak up the rays.

A waiter came along – I was his only customer – and I just asked for coffee and biscuits mid-morning and tea and biscuits in the afternoon. I didn't move out of that lovely sun until it was time for lunch or a shower just before we had dinner.

On the Monday we arrived at the city of Miri. As I saw the land come into view I went to find the captain.

'Is it possible to get off and explore?' I asked.

He frowned at me. 'Sorry, no,' he said. 'It's far too dangerous to get that close to the land. There's an enormous sandbank at the bottom.'

This meant the boat couldn't get close enough and we risked running ashore. I was disappointed and it meant a whole three-day wait until we set sail again on the Thursday. So I made the most of reading and sunbathing again.

Finally we set off and reached Labuan just after midnight. This is an island to the north of Brunei Bay and a place of historical interest. Chinese ships had traded here in the sixth and seventh centuries, and it was given to the British by the Sultan of Brunei in 1847 – a memorial stone to Queen Victoria showed this.

In 1942, it had been invaded by the Japanese and was under occupation for three and a half years. By all accounts the locals suffered terribly, with their homes and livelihoods devastated by bombings and fires, but it had now been rebuilt and I couldn't wait to get on land to explore.

After breakfast, I carefully stepped off the boat and set off on my own. First I went and looked at points of interest in Victoria and then stopped at a café to get a cold drink.

I was vaguely aware of people, especially men, looking at me, but I shrugged off the stares and just concentrated on what I was doing. A group of taxis arrived nearby, so I decided to pay a driver to show me around the island. I only had a few hours to spare while the cargo was being lifted off.

'Would you show me around the island, please?' I asked one friendly faced cab driver. He beamed with understanding.

'Yes, yes,' he bowed. 'Get in.'

I suppose a small part of me realised I was rather vulnerable – a lone woman, jumping into a cab on an island in the middle of nowhere with nobody knowing where I was – but again I just shrugged it off. I was too excited to see this little-known territory and just wanted to get on with it!

He stopped off at points of interest and then turned to me. 'You go graves now,' he said.

I nodded. I wasn't sure if war graves were something I longed to see, but I let him carry on with his self-made tour.

As we turned down the road where the cemetery lay, I gasped. It was overwhelmingly beautiful, with trees and flowers of every description and colour hanging everywhere. I stepped out of the car into the cool of the shade, looking at row upon row of immaculate white headstones.

All the British names seemed to leap out at me, their

dates of birth and death so close together, it made me want to weep. I thought of George . . . as I always did really. 'Where are you?' I half-murmured to myself. I swallowed hard and closed my eyes, breathing in the scent and listening to the sound of birds. For a resting place it was fit for a king and was nothing less than our boys deserved.

I wandered around and saw the graves were of the dead of the Commonwealth forces. It was as well kept as any major botanical garden and I felt comforted to think these graves were so well tended, and here I was now, having my own chance to pay some respects to these terribly brave men. Afterwards, my cabbie showed me the memorial stone just off the beach commemorating where the commander of the Ninth Division Australian Forces received the unconditional surrender of the Japanese army in 1945.

As we walked away I spotted a couple of people stooped on the shore with nets.

'What are they doing?' I asked, pointing. The cabbie beckoned me over to speak to them. As we arrived, I saw the elderly figures turn and smile at me, with toothless grins, their faces full of lines. They were women, both fishing.

They gabbled at me in their own languages, looking so happy and carefree. I could hardly believe it, and once again I realised just how far away I'd come from my life in the stuffy convent.

All too soon, it was time to go back to the boat.

'There you go,' I said, peeling off many more dollars than I needed to. 'Thank you so much for your help.'

He'd behaved like a perfect gentleman and I suppose now

I was back I realised how relieved I was.

Back on board, we set sail again, this time to Kota Kina-balu, the capital of Sabah, a Westernised town cooled by the breeze of the South China Sea and the place our boat had taken its name from.

Before I went to get off the boat again, I looked in the mirror. Gasping, I had to laugh. The walnut-coloured face peering back at me was almost unrecognisable. My hair was a mass of knots and frizz.

'Oh dear, Win,' I muttered to myself. 'Even in the middle of nowhere, you're not walking around like that!' I hadn't had the nerve to use the precious water supply on the boat to sort out my barnet myself, so when I hopped off the boat I headed straight into town to find a hairdresser, and I had my usual set and tidy-up.

Afterwards, I went back to the boat to re-read a guide book and decide where else I'd like to see. I'd heard about the Kadazan girls in a town called Papar, twenty-four miles away, by the river. It was the centre of the rice-growing district and these girls were known to be some of the most attractive in the world. I was also amazed to read the town used to be full of indigenous people who hunted heads, but thankfully now they'd turned their hands to agriculture and rice-growing.

I mentioned my idea to one of the men over lunch. A few of them piped up then.

'Oh, you want to go to Papar,' they said. 'It's an incredible place.' After hearing more and more of them chime in about the wonders, my mind was made up.

'I'm going, then!' I smiled.

They all cheered. 'You won't regret it,' they laughed.

I set off for a bus station and stood waiting for an hour for one to Papar. But none seemed to be coming. Then a Chinese gentleman approached me.

'Where you going?' he asked.

'Papar,' I said.

He looked shocked. 'You cannot go at this time. No time for a lady to be going on her own to Papar. It's too late. You come for a drink with me instead?'

I quickly shook my head. 'Sorry,' I said, politely. 'Actually, I'd better get back after all. The captain of my ship will be wondering where I am.'

I was relieved to get away and so glad I had the excuse of the captain behind me. It was a good way of discouraging people – especially men – from causing me any trouble.

Chapter Twenty

The High Life

The next morning I woke up early and tried again. I was still determined to get to Papar! This time I waited and a bus turned up with a big sign saying 'PAPAR' so I hopped on and sat at the back of the bus. I was aware a single white woman might attract attention so I wanted to keep a low profile.

As I made myself comfortable, I fanned my face with my hat and looked up. There, already, were a group of local men, all sitting turned in their seats to face me, their elbows resting on the seat in front.

'Hallo, laydeee,' they all said, grinning.

I sighed. Fat chance I'd get any peace then! I just smiled politely and turned my head to look out of the window, hoping they'd get bored of looking. I know I'd had my hair done, but really there wasn't much to see!

I concentrated on the view outside and watched as shanty towns gave way to green hills in the distance. The road colour soon changed to red and plumes of red dust rose as the wheels of the bus whizzed round, sending up clouds into the window and all over me. I coughed and spluttered and was pleased when we finally stopped two hours later. I jumped off to find a quiet-looking town.

'No market day today,' the driver told me in broken English.

'Are the Kadazan women around?' I asked.

He shook his head. 'No ladies today.'

I couldn't believe it! I'd come all this way for nothing. So I just sat and waited an hour for the next bus to take me home again.

I arrived back in Kota Kinabalu and went into a nearby restaurant to have a good meal before heading back to the boat. Once again I glanced in the mirror and laughed. This time I was covered from head to toe in a fine, red dust.

I washed my arms up to my elbows and then, looking almost more ridiculous, sat down with white arms and a red body for something to eat.

Back on the boat, the lads fell about laughing looking at me. 'Did you make it to Papar?' they asked.

'Yes,' I said, 'but it was all closed. What did you see when you went there?'

They roared with laughter. 'Nothing!' one said. 'None of us have ever been!'

I knew they were taking the mickey now, but just laughed along with them.

I spent ages in the shower, trying to get rid of the dust. My new hairstyle was completely ruined as well. But at least I'd tried to see something!

Over dinner that evening, I got chatting to the captain.

'You amaze me, Phill,' he said. 'I mean, I've never ever met a woman who is as completely liberated as you are . . . you go everywhere on your own. Nothing stops you.'

I agreed. 'It's not something I've ever thought about,' I replied. 'But you're right.'

I hated the idea of being thought of as a 'women's libber'. I'd heard about all the changes and campaigns to bring in equal rights back home, which was all well and good. But the fact was, I felt perfectly equal to any man already. I'd joined the army. I went travelling. I did whatever pleased me. And I didn't think beyond that.

On the last day of my journey, I spent the day watching the rubber and rice supplies being stowed back in the hold and catching a few last rays of sun. I was so pleased I'd come on this trip, despite missing some of the sights.

Back on dry land, one of the other crew members helping us off looked at me with a puzzled expression.

'You Spanish?' he asked.

I laughed out loud. 'No! I am as English as they come!' I giggled. I was so brown, people genuinely didn't know who I was.

Back in the mess, everyone commented on how tanned I was. The girls were so jealous. 'You look like a native,' they said.

'Ah, it'll all wash off within a week or so,' I replied. And it did!

I was happy to be back, getting into the swing of things in the office again. I prided myself on being efficient and as cheery as possible.

One day though, the Major came striding in with a file to be sorted. He came and spoke to us all in turn and then paused at my desk before he went into the Brigadier's office.

'Marry me, Phill, will you?' he muttered to me, as he caught my eye sweeping past.

I was just about to sign off some paperwork and dropped my pen in shock. I watched as his back disappeared into the Brigadier's office. I was flabbergasted.

I turned to the chief clerk, who was also sat gaping like a goldfish.

'Did . . . did . . . you just hear what I heard?' I said. 'Or did I imagine that?' The look on his face told me he most certainly had done.

'Yep,' he replied. 'I couldn't work out whether he's being cheeky or what!'

I laughed. Neither could I. But I wasn't even going to entertain the idea. Even though I had long since lost my fear of mixing with higher ranks, I definitely knew this Major wasn't my 'type', and if he was going to ask me on a date he'd need to do a better job than that!

A few months later though, something did come up. The Major was briskly walking into the office to collect some paperwork when he asked me something else.

'I'm going to join the former Sultan of Brunei for a polo match,' he said. 'Would you care to join me?'

'Yes, sir,' I replied without hesitation. I didn't know what his motives were in this, but I'd never been to see polo before.

We arrived at the event, filled with local dignitaries, and not many British. The Major was a perfect gentleman all day and I was relieved to see he wasn't trying anything with me.

He even introduced me to the recently abdicated Sultan himself. I was so shocked when I saw him. The pictures I'd seen of him had always been in newspapers and he'd been a suave, good-looking chap. This bloated, middle-aged man in front of me looked nothing like him. I politely shook his hand. I marvelled at how he was so very rich but didn't look wealthy at all, the way he was very simply dressed in white linen.

'Pleased to meet you,' I said.

I was excited inside, thinking of little old me at a polo match, shaking hands with a sultan. But this soon wore off as the game started. I loved watching the beautiful horses but couldn't get as excited as the Major did as they ran around the pitch. After several hours I was struggling to hide my yawns.

Despite this disappointing experience, there were plenty of other fascinating trips I made in my final few months in Singapore.

One place we went to was the RAF base in Changi. One of the rooms had been cornered off as it was home to six incredible paintings of religious scriptures. They really were stunning to look at, and officers had decided to protect them. They had been discovered a few years earlier when decorating was in progress, and underneath the top paint the pictures were found.

Nobody knew who'd done them or the story behind them until an officer suggested asking a journalist to help out, and the Major wrote to the *Daily Mirror* asking them to make an appeal.

Unbelievably, the artist got in touch. Bombardier Stanley Warren had been a prisoner of war in Changi Prison and was in the hospital suffering from renal disease and malnutrition. I shuddered when I heard the details.

'He'd got kidney stones,' said one of the officers, 'and his life was in danger so the other lads decided to operate.'

'Ouch!' I winced. 'Using what exactly?'

'Well it says here,' said the officer, squinting at the text, 'they hadn't any drugs or disinfectants but managed to safely removed the stones with a knife.'

I clamped my hands over my ears. 'Say no more!' I cried.

But the rest of the story was just incredible. While he lay recovering from his operation, Warren heard some of the Australian prisoners singing a litany in the nearby chapel, and he found it so uplifting that when he made his miraculous recovery, he decided to show his appreciation by painting. He begged the boys to steal him as many paints and brushes around the camp as they could.

And then he set to work, night after night, spending hours by candlelight on the paintings of Christ and stories from the scriptures on the wall of the chapel of block 151.

The place became a haven for the POWs and they all loved the paintings, as we did all these years later. They were almost destroyed though by the Japanese when they painted over it, but in 1958 they were uncovered again. The room had been used as a store but then one day it was being cleaned for use as a billet when the colours of the mural emerged in all their glory.

Warren was by now an art master in a London school and in 1963 was even persuaded to come back to Changi to restore the murals. He repainted the fourth mural but left the fifth untouched as a memorial to his original work. He also painted an albatross as a tribute to the RAF in one of them.

Almost everyone who came to Singapore went to visit these extraordinary paintings at one time or another. I've never seen the like since.

Another last-minute trip I went on was to Chinatown, the side of Singapore I'd missed in previous visits. It was the 'unseen' side where tourists rarely ventured. We took a side turning down streets I'd never visited before to find the 'Hakka women'; these poor hard-working ladies toiled in building sites, carrying out heavy work usually only done by men. Their job was to build houses for the very poor and 'death' houses. These were terribly sad places where old folk who'd lost their family paid just a dollar or so to rent a single room, where they lived out their final days.

It was seen as a step up though, as previously the old could just be left out on the street to die.

Nearby were many funeral parlours. Although deaths were frequent there was always a ritual carried out afterwards. And they would build an effigy of whatever the deceased had been in life. While there I was amazed to see a beautifully made rickshaw fashioned out of paper.

'You'll never guess what this gentleman did,' chuckled our guide.

'Rickshaw driver?' I hazarded a guess.

'Correct,' he said. Along with the paper transport, paper money was also burned. This was to ensure the old had something to spend in the afterlife.

I thought it was a strange idea in a way. It looked as if almost more time was spent on these poor old folk when they were dead rather than alive.

We were warned not to approach some of the houses as they were full of 'opium addicts'. But as the guide carried on in front of us, a few of us lingered behind.

'Hey, quick!' said one of the girls I was with. We ducked into a house and peered around the doorway. It was another rather sad and pathetic sight to see old folk hunched around a pipe, billows of smoke rising from their heads.

Despite all these fascinating times, I really had started to long to leave the army. I was coming to the end of my twenty-two years' service and it had been a blast. But ultimately being constantly told where to go and what to do does take its toll. Even the most patriotic of servicemen and women cannot help feel like their freedom is beckoning.

I also wanted to spend the last six months of my service back in the UK if possible. I wanted to start to rebuild a life in civvy street, look for somewhere to live and plan my new life . . . out of the army.

* * *

Finally I was given permission to go home. So I started spending more of my spare time shopping for household goods and packing them ready to send home, things like crockery and the odd bit of furniture – things I'd never had to consider buying before. Then one morning I was summoned to see the OC. His next plan for me was very surprising.

'We would like you to go to the British Embassy in Djakarta to relieve the Warrant Officer working there while he's on home leave for six weeks.'

'Really!' I gasped. Then I remembered myself and stood straight and nodded. 'With pleasure,' I said.

As usual, I couldn't resist the chance of going to see another country. Even better if it was one with a strange name I'd never heard of!

I was told I'd be on the next plane over there, the one used by the ambassador no less. That was certainly a step up from a cargo ship.

The next morning at breakfast in the mess, the girls left me a scroll of paper.

'What's this?' I asked, unfurling it.

Someone had drawn me a cartoon of the ambassador's plane with my little suitcase attached by a piece of string hanging off it.

'Ha ha ha!' I laughed, as the table of people melted into giggles. 'Very funny.'

'We hope they actually let you sit on the plane, Phill,' said someone.

'Me too,' I smiled.

The plane was a small one, a Dove, just a tiny four-seater. By now I'd overcome my fear of flying. I was shown on board and where the toilets were (although you couldn't miss them) and we set off, with just myself, the pilot, navigator and a flight sergeant.

I sat back and relaxed, munching on sandwiches and coffee as I admired the view.

We flew at just 600 feet over the island of Sumatra, the sixth largest island in the world. It was incredible, looking down at the jungle and seeing the rivers winding through them like snakes between the trees. As we approached Java, we saw some of the smaller islands off the coast, looking like jewels of green nestled in the brilliant blue sea. In the distance I could see some ominous black clouds, billowing in the sky further away. I was so glad we seemed to be flying away from them.

We landed with a little bump and I emerged blinking into the sunshine, feeling as though I'd stepped into a boiling-hot oven. It was so much hotter than Singapore even.

'Thank you,' I said to the captain. 'I'm glad we missed the black clouds.'

He grinned. 'It was a monsoon,' he said. 'And because we had a lady on board I decided we'd better navigate round them rather than straight through.'

'Well, I'm grateful for your thoughtfulness, sir,' I cried.

The embassy was a modern building, as it had been rebuilt following the riots and uprising in the early 1960s. I was shown to my desk and saw the remnants of the troubles. My typewriter still had sooty burn marks streaking the sides of it from flames when the previous building had been torched, but it still worked so had been saved!

I was introduced to everyone there and the embassy wives were very welcoming, bringing me a large bouquet of flowers. The doctor also came to say hello.

'I hope I don't need to see you again,' I chuckled, shaking his hand. 'And I mean that in the nicest possible way.'

I was to stay in the Warrant Officer's home. It was very large and comfy, but so hot I couldn't get a good night's sleep. I also couldn't work out how to use the antiquated hot-water system. It ran on a geyser you needed to fill with kerosene, but try as I might I couldn't work it out, so just settled for cold water to wash in.

There were two lady servants, known as amahs, who were at my beck and call. This felt a little uncomfortable as I wasn't used to people wanting to help me every few minutes. I enquired how much they were getting paid.

'You cannot pay them anything extra,' I was warned.

But I couldn't face thinking how little they probably earned for all their hard work. So when I could I'd slip to the local market and buy them a colourful sari or two to make up for their low wages.

They really treated me like a queen. At the end of each hot day a glass of cold beer would be waiting for me.

'This is worth a million pounds,' I said gratefully, as I gulped it down.

There was also a night-watchman assigned to watch over my house for me. However, I used to peer out of my window at night to hear him snoring loudly, fast asleep on the lawn.

Occasionally I'd be woken by his loud hacking cough, which did nothing to help me sleep either! I knew he was about as much use as a guard cat, but at the same time, I was warned if he wasn't there I'd very likely be burgled. So he acted as a deterrent if nothing else.

One morning I woke up and looked out onto the lawn to see it teeming with little animals.

'There are so many cats outside running around,' I said to my amah.

She laughed loudly. 'They are not cats, missy, they are rats!' she cried.

I couldn't believe how big the little horrors were.

At weekends I had a female driver called Andre to show me around the area. There was so much to see I was spoiled for choice. West Java is a mountainous region but the northern half is occupied by a broad plain and is used to plant rice, producing 3 million tons a year nowadays. Tea plantations cover 450,000 acres, producing 50,000 tons a year. We certainly weren't going to run out of either on this island. The other commonly produced product was quinine. This was used to fight malaria and even though a synthetic cure had been produced, most Indonesians still used it.

One day Andre suggested a trip to a tea plantation. It was a sight I will never forget. We stopped at a café on the Puncak Pass where we saw the view across the plains below the sun and the clouds, which threw a beautiful pattern across the land. There we saw hundreds of women, hunched over, with shawls on and a basket on their backs, nimbly picking the leaves and tossing them in their baskets.

My heart clenched as I watched them soundlessly shuffling along. The scene was so peaceful and quite beautiful. But also very sad. I knew they were being paid a pittance. Really they were little more than slaves and their lives were bound by this work. In comparison I was as free as a bird and so lucky to be living the life that I was.

Another sight I couldn't resist seeing was the volcano Tangkuban Perahu. So Andre, her husband and I went to Bandung and stayed overnight in a motel before rising very early.

Trees on the way up to the volcano were disturbingly scorched and blackened. I shuddered.

'Are you sure it won't erupt,' I half joked.

'Don't worry, missy,' said Andre. 'They close the road to cars if there is any chance.'

I wondered how fail-safe it was knowing when an eruption was on the cards.

The smell was terrible too as our car became smothered in yellow, sulphurous dust. 'Rotten eggs!' we all groaned, holding our noses.

Finally we came to a stop and all got out, the smell and the heat hitting me immediately. In silence we crept up to the edge of a cavernous hole where it bubbled menacingly on the other side.

'Urgh, goodness,' I gasped. 'I think that's near enough for me.'

I couldn't believe it when I saw people walking towards the bubbling. I stood and looked at the view of the countryside sweeping majestically in all colours before us as the mist descended.

'What a vision,' I murmured to Andre.

We couldn't stop for long as mist was already collecting and soon we'd be engulfed. So we started our slow and careful climb back down.

In the car on the way back, I saw and watched as so many scenes flew by the window; carts pulled by oxen, horse-drawn cabs, rice stacked like hayricks, women washing clothes in the river . . . Once again I thought how far away from Coventry all this was.

Djakarta itself was a heaving mix of rich and poor. I'll never forget the sight of a poor man covered in absolutely nothing except for a worn plastic sheet, scrabbling on a rubbish tip looking for food or something to sell . . . and then in the background a huge monument topped by an imitation flame made from pure gold, worth millions probably. There was something quite uncomfortable and sickening about it.

By now, I was quite used to living this high life and my weight was creeping up massively. I loved the food in Singapore and Djarkata was just as good. I found it impossible to turn down some of the delicacies, like frog legs and the infamous rijsttafel, which means 'rice table'. This was given the name by Dutch settlers who also loved the rich spices and experimented with them, adding them to all kinds of chicken and rice dishes.

With food like this it was so hard to resist, and I ignored my skirt waistband slowly tightening!

* * *

I'd had a sore throat for a while and started to develop a rather husky voice so, back in Singapore after my relief stint in Djakarta, I went to the doctor and he diagnosed laryngitis. But, looking me up and down, he said something else.

'Phill, get on those scales now,' he said.

I hopped on and could hardly bear to look. I knew I'd piled on weight over the past year or so.

'You're thirteen stone!' he gasped. 'Right, this needs sorting out.'

He scribbled on some paper and ordered me to take it to the Sergeants' mess caterer so he could make me special meals. From now on I was being put on a special diet, mainly of fish and veg.

I couldn't complain, as I knew I'd grown too big. At my farewell dinner though, I still wasn't allowed what everyone else was having. So while they tucked into a roast turkey I was made to eat fish and salad.

On the last Saturday in June the day had arrived for me to leave Singapore. I had such mixed feelings. I stood outside the mess, my face in the sunshine, thinking of what lay in store for me. I knew I'd miss the sun and the warmth so much. Although I longed to go home on the one hand, on the other I didn't miss the grey skies and rain of England one bit.

I ran a few more errands before saying goodbye to everyone again. The General and his wife sent me an invitation to the wedding of their son, who was to be married later in the year in the crypt of St Paul's Cathedral.

I went and bought a few final gifts, including a box of orchids for my brother Ken's wife. They cost a fortune and filled a very long awkward box, but I couldn't resist as I knew how much Phyllis would love them.

After a few more handshakes and even a tear, I was waved off for my plane home. Back to reality.

Chapter Twenty-one

Goodbye to the Army

Back on British soil, the main thing that struck me was how different the men looked! In Singapore if any man had tried to enter with hair like that he'd have been given short shrift and sent out for a haircut. So many now sported untidy long hair. There were strange wide-legged trousers everywhere too – someone told me they were called flares – and lots of thick-soled shoes.

Once again I just shrugged my shoulders when it came to fashion. My wardrobe still consisted only of my uniform with the odd dress to go out dancing in.

I was stationed back in Mill Hill and as my car drove me there, I felt so empty. The streets all looked so grey, matching the colour of the skies, and not knowing where I was going to end up didn't help my mood.

I also couldn't believe how much London had changed. There were cars and people everywhere, it seemed twice as busy, with faces from every ethnicity.

One day I tried to go for a walk around my old haunts near Rutland Gate and Hyde Park but even that looked different. It seemed like a busy, manic air had filled the city.

Somehow it felt more threatening and dangerous. I was now a stranger in my own town.

Work wasn't any more fun really, and it seemed a shame to see out my army days feeling rather despondent and bored. I did find a letter once in a file though, which showed me how appreciated my work had been, even if I found it hard to feel the same sense of satisfaction. It was from the embassy in Djakarta, thanking the Major.

I am writing to thank you for allowing WO II Phillips to come over to Djakarta as a temporary relief for my assistant . . . She fitted into the rather strange routine of the Embassy remarkably quickly and smoothly and impressed everyone from the Ambassador down by her cheerfulness, efficiency, and willingness to accept the many unfamiliar tasks that were thrust upon her. She is clearly a very high grade PA and a thoroughly pleasant person to work with.

I went up to visit my brother and his wife and had a chat with Ken about my future. I'd loved army life but felt it had come to its natural end. I longed to make my own decisions and not be 'told' what to do. But how I would go about starting again, I'd no idea!

'You know, Win, everyone who leaves the army finds it hard at first, but I've no doubt you'll find your way,' Ken said.

I'd heard this many times before. In the army you had a sense of belonging, you knew your life was mapped out before you. I felt like I'd thrown the compass away.

'I know,' I said. 'I just need to find a new way now.'

I decided then and there to rent a small flat in Norfolk so I had somewhere to stay at the weekends. I wanted to get out of the Big Smoke as much as possible. I caught the train back to London feeling glummer than ever, and decided now my twenty-two years were coming up I'd apply to leave.

Leaving the army is as simple an affair as signing up in the end. I simply typed a letter asking to resign and handed it in. Anyone could unless they were in the secret service or other special duties.

When news got out I was going, people did show their sadness.

'It's a shame, Phill,' said my NCO. But she understood. I was forty-four now and ready to start again. Even if I didn't know exactly what to do!

I was given the due date of January 1971, when I was to be demobbed for the last time. Now I had a firm date I set the wheels in motion for my new life and decided to buy a bungalow in Norfolk. I'd always been a regular saver with my building society and was allowed a mortgage.

On my final day in London, I packed up and handed in my neatly washed and pressed uniform and all my passes. I also packed my medals. So far I had the Malaya Medal with a bar on it to indicate my time in Cyprus, one for Singapore, and my Malaya Peninsular Medal for good conduct (really that means you've never been caught!). Later on I was to get a medal from the King of Malaysia too. I never got one for Egypt, I'm not sure why. Medals really show where you have served and I got more than many of the boys did.

There were a few tears and hugs, but most of my friends had left long ago. I was still in touch with them and that's all that mattered. Civvy street had beckoned and I was going to go for it.

In May, on a boiling hot day, I was handed the keys to my bungalow. If I was being honest I didn't particularly like Norfolk with its flat, barren countryside and bogs. It had a desolate air and was a world away from the lush vegetation in Singapore I'd so loved. But Ken was there and I knew there were a few job prospects. It was a place to at least lay my head for a while. It was a small, neat place and I couldn't believe I'd finally done it. When the estate agent handed me the keys I tossed them into the air, catching them and smiling.

'I'll have my own front door for the first time,' I murmured.

I quickly applied for jobs in the area and got offered one in a solicitor's office as a secretary.

My first day back at work was the strangest. To be wearing smart civvies and just starting again felt a bit like being the new girl at school.

The solicitor, Mr Jackson, was a lazy man. He was rarely in the office and always seemed to be having lie-ins or was hard to get hold of. I was so used to the busy bustle of army life and the discipline it came with, this was hard to take.

He got me to run all kinds of errands, including family ones. Once his mother rang up to ask him something or other and he expected me to deal with this too.

'Can you please sort out some files for me, before I take the call?' he asked. It was something to do with a legal matter for his family, so I looked in his safe for some paperwork pertaining to a house mortgage.

As I read his address, my eyes widened.

'St Martin's Road, Canterbury,' it read.

Surely not! I thought. And I asked him if that was really where he'd lived.

'Yes,' he said.

'Well, so did I!' I cried. 'My Auntie Annie lived there for years.'

Mr Jackson's face brightened. 'I knew Annie,' he said. 'And Percy and George and Maisie . . . I don't remember you though.'

It was my turn to smile wryly now. 'I was often away at boarding school,' I said.

Afterwards I called Maisie and asked her if she also remembered Mr Jackson.

'I certainly do,' she said. 'I even remember taking him out in the pram when he was a wee baby.'

I laughed at what a small world we live in. Although we found this unexpected thing in common, we had little else. I grew tired of having to run errands for this rather lazy, inefficient man.

He could be very rude too. Just before he was about to take two weeks' holiday, we had a row about a case of his.

'You don't know what you're doing,' he said rudely.

I looked up from my typing and glared at him but as I glanced up he'd already picked up a book.

Raising it above his head, he slung it at me as hard as possible.

I couldn't quite register what I was seeing as it sailed through the air, landing in a heap on the floor as I quickly dodged it.

In a flash I'd picked it up.

'Who do you think you're yelling at?' I cried back, picking it up and throwing it back at him. He stormed out of the office, as I sat at my desk in disbelief. I just knew then and there I couldn't go on like this.

That afternoon I packed up my things, and when he returned from holiday I was no longer there. I'd already typed out my resignation, and left it on his desk.

Back in my house, I closed my front door and sat in the living room. All I could hear was the clock ticking and the fridge humming. It felt so quiet and for the first time I realised just how alone I felt too.

In the army you're always surrounded by people. You might not necessarily like them, but you always had someone there. If anyone fell down they were automatically helped up. In fact, now I realised all my life I'd been surrounded by people – from boarding school onwards it was all I knew.

In civvy street I was remembering again this wasn't always the case. I had to sort things out on my own, and although I'd never been one to feel lonely, it seemed this was the case now.

I decided to make a new move and start again in Shropshire, near my brother Norman who was still working as a policeman in Shrewsbury. This seemed like a sensible idea. It was near some beautiful countryside, which I loved.

I also made a rash decision to go back to nursing, at least to try it again. Although I'd never liked it years ago, I hoped NHS nursing might be a little different. So I got a job as an auxiliary nurse at a hospital in Ironbridge. I'd forgotten what hard work it was, but after being so bored at the solicitor's I was pleased to get stuck in.

The wards were huge and very busy. I mainly worked on wards with elderly folk and someone was always dying or needing attention. It was relentless. I remembered just how much I disliked those jobs, such as polishing their bedpans until they shone, but at the same time I loved the sense of camaraderie and some of the patients. I happily pushed them around in their wheelchairs, even to the pub sometimes or wherever they wanted to go.

The work was physically draining though, and I found the bones in my hands started to hurt like crazy. Doctors had a look and tests revealed I had developed rheumatoid arthritis.

'I am afraid you'll never recover from this,' I was warned.

Thankfully though I did, even though the pain killed me for a time, especially when I had to try and do heavy jobs like bathing the men on the ward. I was at the hospital for three years and was grateful to receive a pension after I left. The hospital had turned into a private hospital and I wasn't happy about carrying on there.

*　　*　　*

In 1982, I got a phone call from Ken.

'Listen, Win, he said, 'I got a phone call this morning from Southport Hospital to say Mum has died. They want someone to go and sort out all of her things and the funeral. Phyll and I are just off to Japan for a holiday. I really don't want to miss it, would you mind sorting this out?'

The news Mum had died was a bit of a shock, even though I knew by now she'd be eighty-five. But at the same time there was no sadness; I'd not seen her for many years now. Ken wasn't in the least bit saddened either. The woman who'd given us up all those years ago was little more than a stranger now.

'OK, Ken,' I said. 'I'll deal with it.'

I rang Norman and Cliff and both of them just huffed on the phone. They couldn't have cared less and really I didn't blame them. We all felt the same about this woman.

But the arrangements had to be made, so I went up to the hospital. The sister there shook my hand and greeted me with the tenderness a daughter would normally get for the loss of her mother.

'Would you like to see her now?' she said softly.

I shook my head. 'No thank you,' I said politely.

Her eyebrows shot up in surprise. 'But why not?'

'I don't want to,' I replied.

'You don't wish to go and see your own mother?' she asked, a little quietly.

I shook my head. 'She was no mother to me . . . or any of us,' I said sadly.

I was very efficient in signing the death certificate and then was given the keys to her room at her hospice so I could sort through her things. Entering her little room, all of her belongings, clothes, pictures, books and papers had already been neatly placed into boxes.

I looked through some of them. There wasn't a single sign of my mother having had any children at all. No photographs. None of our childhood belongings. Nothing.

I bundled up her things in bin bags to go to the charity shop and then made arrangements for a funeral, organising a coffin and cremation.

She hadn't left a will but legally we had to deal with it, so I agreed to be the executor, signing all the relevant documents and informing the bank of her death. I found myself doing it mechanically, and just wanted the job done. I divided up what little she did have between myself and my brothers. Both Norman and Ken told me to keep the money, they didn't want anything from her, but Cliff happily took his cheque and said, 'Thank you very much.'

On the day of her funeral none of us went. It would have seemed silly to do so.

Epilogue

And so, once again, I found myself longing to move on. By 1999, I decided to move from Shropshire to Deal in Kent to be near Maisie's children, especially Jenny her daughter, who I got on very well with, and I finally moved into some sheltered accommodation. I certainly still felt as fit as a fiddle, but realised I might not always feel this way.

After spending the intervening years in a variety of hospital and civil service jobs, by now I had retired and I found myself with more time on my hands; once again my thoughts turned to George. I suppose actually I'd never stopped thinking about him, but now it played on my mind that I'd never got to the bottom of what happened to him. And I had time to do something about it.

My family had always known my story with George. Often I found myself wistfully wondering about him, if we saw anything relevant on news or TV. So much time had passed but I knew perhaps records could show now what had happened to him. My cousin Kathleen Phillips, who lived in Croydon and who I still kept in touch with, made a helpful suggestion one day.

'I was reading there is a huge memorial of all the RAF serviceman who were still missing engraved in an archway in Runnymede,' she said. 'I'll take you down there if you like and have a look to see if we can spot the name George Wheeler.'

'Would you?' I exclaimed. 'I really would love to start doing something to see if I can find him, but I just don't know where to start.'

We drove up there one sunny day and walked over to the arch. Peering carefully, we looked down alphabetically to the Ws but straight away I realised there was no 'George Wheeler' there at all.

'Oh, Win,' said Kathleen. 'He's not here, is he?'

'No,' I sighed. 'Plenty more are though . . .'

Although they were just names of strangers chipped in stone we were looking at, to me, I knew how much heartache must lie behind each loss. Years of wondering, years of pain, and in many cases a complete diversion in the paths of those they left behind. I knew there were hundreds of women like me, who'd never married after losing the one they'd really wanted.

Now I'd made an effort to look though, I decided to take my efforts further. It had been a question all of my life and now was my chance to finally solve it. I felt in a way I owed it to George to find out.

I decided to write to the War Graves Commission, to ask them for help. A few weeks later they replied saying they could report that a George Wheeler was buried in Berlin.

As I held the letter, I found myself staring at the words, and re-reading it. After all these years, although I realised of course he must be dead, this was finally someone confirming it.

It had taken me over fifty years just to see it in black and white.

The next step was to contact the War Graves Commission again, who could help people go on trips to find graves. So I did so and arranged to go with them.

It felt rather strange to be away on what looked like a holiday to do something so sad, so serious. But in my mind I was firm; it needed to be done.

It was a cold day when I boarded a coach to drive to Berlin, a long, tedious journey, but with lots of jolly people on board, also looking for loved ones. Finally we arrived at a cemetery, I forget what it was called, and once more my heart clenched as I spotted row after row of white headstones, all carefully tended on immaculate lawns. All those bodies, all those young men. I just couldn't even reconcile myself with what a complete waste it was of their lives.

And in some cases of those they left behind too.

I was led by our guide using a map to find George's neat headstone. But as I approached and the lettering came into view, I knew instantly it wasn't him. Part of me felt like we were in the wrong place anyway, but looking at those words, I knew it.

On this grave was 'George Wheeler' but written below was: 'Bomb Aimer'.

'No!' I gasped, making my guide jump a little. 'I'm sorry, but no, this is not George's grave.'

'Are you sure?' he said.

'Yes I am,' I nodded. 'My George was a wireless operator not a bomb aimer.'

He peered at the stone and read it for himself.

'I'm sorry, you're probably right then,' he said.

I shivered. 'I knew it wasn't his grave when we arrived,' I said sadly. 'I don't know how, but I knew.'

We walked slowly away, and I felt so let down. These mistakes were so easily made while looking for graves. There were so very many dead, keeping track was impossible.

Back home, I felt more determined than ever now to uncover the truth. I also discovered an organisation called The War Research Society, started by serving and retired armed forces members and policemen to take widows, children and veterans to find the war graves of their loved ones. So I sat down and wrote a letter asking for help. Unfortunately, they said they didn't have any more access to records than the War Graves Commission had done. They were very kind though.

'Once you find him, let us know and we'll take you there,' they said.

I was touched by how people wanted to help.

I rang them to explain my situation further and they suggested I join a tour. I started to lose hope a little now and didn't know who to turn to. 'Maybe I'm destined never to find him,' I said to Kathleen, although I didn't want to believe that. After all, George *must* be somewhere if he wasn't listed as missing. I had faith after all these years that all the lads who died were accounted for.

As a last resort I decided to use my own connections with the army. As an ex-Warrant Officer I hoped it would hold some sway and I wrote a long and polite letter to the RAF asking for their help.

'We will most certainly have a look,' they said. 'Although I am sure you appreciate there are so many graves and records to go through.'

I did appreciate this, but I was desperate. Any help they could give was better than nothing.

A few weeks later, I got another letter. I opened it carefully, this time sitting down with a cup of tea. I knew if they didn't know what happened to George, probably nobody would.

As I opened it, the words just felt like knives. Sadly, I have lost the actual letter, but I can clearly remember what it said:

'We can inform you that George Wheeler died in an aeroplane crash overnight in July 1944, in France after being hit by enemy fire while returning from Stuttgart on a bombing mission. All seven crew died after being burned to death when their plane exploded. It had been one of George's last sorties before his leave. The bodies were buried by local French people who saw the crash. Later officials returned to dig up the bodies for reburial in the cathedral cemetery and after the war the War Graves Commission returned to exhume their bodies again to rebury them in the appropriate war graves cemetery.'

Tears, as if it had happened just yesterday, pricked in my eyes. Thoughts of George and his gentle manner, his words, his letters, his kisses, all came flooding into my memory as fresh as if I were that seventeen-year-old girl again.

'Oh, George,' I said out loud to myself. I looked at my hands, holding the letter, now rather elderly-looking and shaking. The grief was still there. I was still here. But I'd done it. I'd found him. I knew damn well I'd find it so very sad, but I'd done it.

I wrote back to the research society asking if they were still able to take me to see George. They quickly wrote back to say they'd be delighted to help and one of their guides, Ian, could assist me.

So I found myself packing again and on another coach tour, this time to the Commonwealth cemetery in Lisieux, a town in northern France that was two-thirds destroyed during one bombardment a month before George's plane was shot down.

We wandered into the cemetery. This time, I knew it was exactly where George's remains were, thanks to the research and Ian's map, and it was overwhelming.

'I've waited so long to do this,' I said to Ian, my voice breaking.

'I know, Win,' he replied, squeezing my hand. 'And we're right behind you.'

I walked along the now-familiar rows of white headstones, all bearing a name, and so much loss. Then we reached 'W' and there, suddenly, he was.

'George Wheeler. Wireless operator. 25th July 1944.'

It was as if all the decades melted into nothing and my raw grief erupted as though it had been waiting to emerge at the earliest opportunity. My vision grew cloudy with tears as they spilled onto my cheeks.

'Here you are,' I whispered. I bent down to touch the cold, hard headstone, and closed my eyes, allowing myself to think of my boy.

Ian from the War Research Society had already got his camera out and he flicked it on.

'Win,' he said, breathlessly. 'Would you mind possibly just saying a few words into the camera.'

I turned to him, my throat now choking with tears and sobs desperate to emerge.

'I am so sorry,' I croaked. 'I am afraid I just can't.'

He immediately put the camera down and reached to squeeze my hand.

'Of course, Win,' he said. 'Of course.'

I stood swaying for a few moments, feeling the breeze from the trees on my face. Breathing in the air, as George once had. Feeling my feet on the ground, where his lovely bones now lay, perished.

I felt so happy I'd found him. But so utterly bereft all over again.

'Well, I know what happened now, George,' I muttered. And with one last touch, I stroked his headstone and asked if we could go.

On the way out we went to look at the Book of Remembrance. It was filled with spidery writing of loved ones and family members, with a few words about each person.

George's mum and dad had been listed. Their address, however, was now one in Scotland. I closed my eyes and breathed deeply as I remembered the way George's mum hugged me as I stepped over her front door. The way she cooked us those delicious meals. The way she took time to write to me, consoling me for my loss, when she must have been beside herself with grief after losing both her boys. His devastated parents had obviously gone back to their home town, perhaps for a fresh start. Although I know the likelihood was they'd never recovered from their loss.

I spotted an address for them too, but immediately knew I could never try and get in contact. The chances were they were probably dead now too and I couldn't reopen their wounds. I went on a few more tours after that, including to the Somme and Ypres. All of them were moving in their own way. Once I was standing waiting to get back on a coach when someone spotted the medals I was wearing.

'Whose are they, Win?' the gentleman asked. 'Your husband's or your father's?'

'Neither!' I said proudly. 'They are mine!'

One American graveyard was very sad. It was so full up, there wasn't even room for any space in between the headstones.

I also went to see the Bergen-Belsen memorial site, in Lower Saxony in north-western Germany, where 30,000 prisoners died from disease and starvation. I felt I had to make these trips: to see where all the boys ended up, what really happened; to try and gain a sense of what they were going through; but also simply because I wanted to. It was a humbling and fascinating experience and something everyone could learn from.

People joined me from all over the country, some of them looking for their loved ones: brothers, fathers, grandfathers, uncles. A few of them wrote poems and added them to newsletters about the trips. These helped everyone try and make sense of what had happened. The war had ruined so many lives, stolen so many of our loved ones, it was a lot to deal with.

I went to see George's grave once more about two years later. But after that I made the decision not to go again. It really was too upsetting. Today, I still mark the anniversary of his death, 25 July, by always sitting quietly wherever I am, and just remembering. It was a long time ago, a very long time, but it doesn't matter. I will still remember him and feel the loss.

While in Deal I decided to join the Not Forgotten Association. This group was for ex-servicemen and women and I was keen to re-establish old ties and join in the army life again.

Every year we had the bonus of being invited to Buckingham Palace for a garden party. I went about seven or eight times in the end and always had a spare ticket for someone to come with me. One year I took Maisie's daughter, Jenny.

We'd always got on famously and although I'd been alone for many years now, thanks to Maisie and Nora I never felt alone. I always had someone to join me.

This particular year the traffic down The Mall was terrible and we were stuck for ages in a jam, waiting to enter Buckingham Palace. With a mixture of boredom and curiosity we found ourselves peering into other cars to see the other veterans also waiting.

'Hey, isn't that Harry Patch, the famous First World War veteran?' exclaimed Jenny, tapping at her window.

I turned to look and saw a very old gentleman patiently waiting in his seat.

'Ooh, I think it is,' I said.

The wait continued and we adjusted our hats as time ticked on. Suddenly there was a tapping at the window. The driver of the war veteran's car was standing beside ours. Jenny wound her window down.

'Harry just asked me to come over and tell you what beautiful hats you're both wearing.'

We both creased up with giggles.

'Well, thank him very much,' I laughed. We turned to see Harry also shaking with laughter with a cheeky grin on his face. It was so heartening to see how old age needn't dim a person's sense of humour.

At these parties I constantly met up with old girls from all the tours I'd been involved with, from Egypt, Cyprus and Singapore. It was so heartening to see old faces, although I confess, I didn't recognise all of them! We chatted about the good old days, while tucking into strawberries and cream, and cucumber sandwiches.

One year I took my warden from my accommodation in Deal. One of my eyes had grown rheumy and wouldn't stop weeping, so she led me to the paramedic tent for some help. Afterwards I got a certificate to say I'd been treated at Buckingham Palace, and I couldn't resist keeping it for a little memento.

I actually felt rather nervous when the Queen arrived. She was always lovely, but we had to stop mingling and be more wary of who we were talking to. One year, soon after the naked man had jumped security and been found in the palace, I overheard Prince Philip asking one of the Yeomen, 'Did you have a struggle with the naked man at all?' and he tried hard to keep a straight face as he replied, 'It wasn't me who dealt with the incident, sir.'

One day I was reading a copy of the *British Legion* magazine, when I spotted an advert.

'The Chelsea Pensioners home is looking for new occupants.' The advert went on to say the entry conditions needed to be met. The veteran must be no less than sixty-five years of age, and needed to surrender their pension in exchange for board and lodgings. My eyes lit up.

I immediately remembered the smart old gentlemen, always around in Knightsbridge, who'd occasionally come and visit our mess there. They'd seemed so happy, content, I suppose. And then it occurred to me . . . I wondered if women were also allowed.

For me, sexism was something I never stopped long enough to notice and wasn't something I wanted to see, so it seemed perfectly fine to write to the governor of the home and make an enquiry to see if I'd be considered.

I was happy enough in Deal but the thought of being back in London, where I'd enjoyed some of my happiest days in Knightsbridge, really appealed. Besides, I wasn't getting any fitter and I knew to be cared for at the Royal Hospital would be a real honour and a lovely way to spend my old age.

I also thought of all the men in there too. 'I can chase them around in my wheelchair,' I said cheekily to Jenny when I told her about my idea.

I quickly got a reply, a polite but firm response, informing me that sadly there was no suitable accommodation for women at the Royal Hospital but, the clerk continued, '. . . there is always the Royal Cambridge Home for Widows.'

I'd already heard about this organisation; they provided a care home in East Molesey in Surrey for widows of service-men and also for women who'd served in the army. But I wasn't interested. I wasn't a widow, for a start, and also I preferred the idea of living with men. Looking back, all my life I'd probably got on better with men, I liked the banter. I missed that in my life. I wrote back saying I did know about the Cambridge Home, but if there was any way I could be considered for the Royal Hospital I'd be most happy.

I decided to write every year henceforth, to see if the accommodation situation could be changed in the future. By now I really did have my heart set on it. I just knew I'd end up there . . . somehow!

In 2006, I got a letter from Major General Currie, asking me if I'd mind being put in touch with the BBC, who were keen to make a documentary about the Chelsea Pensioners' home.

They wanted to invite some of the ladies who'd expressed an interest to join, and of course Major General Currie knew I was one of them. They were interested in inviting a few ladies to show us around, with the possibility of sorting out some female-only accommodation, suitable for us. I jumped at the chance.

Arriving on a coach on a chilly autumnal day, we were all very excited. Once again I was struck by the same awe of the building and the history behind it. We learned how the grounds consisted of a bowling green, allotments, library, arts and crafts centre and a billiard room. The chapel was built in 1687 and is used today mainly for Sunday morning worship. The pensioners still parade in the Figure Court, where a statue of King Charles II still stands, and which is the oldest part of the hospital.

On Founder's Day every year the pensioners parade in front of the statue and wear oak leaves, in recognition of the day Charles II restored the monarchy – the oak leaves are a reminder of how he hid in the oak tree from Cromwell's army after the Battle of Worcester in 1651.

The Great Hall stands opposite the chapel and was originally used as a dining room until the end of the eighteenth century, when pensioners ate in their wards instead. The area was used for concerts, recreational pursuit and sometimes even court martials. Then in 1955 it was turned back into a dining room.

We were taken around where the pensioners lived too.

They were set out in long wards divided into berths, each consisting of a bed, table, chair, wardrobe, chest of drawers, and TV and radio. They looked very comfortable, although rather small. There was also an infirmary for the in-pensioners who needed extra care.

All in all I fell in love with the place. It offered such a warm sense of comradeship, something I'd missed since leaving the army.

But we were still warned they'd not got suitable accommodation for women.

It wasn't until January 2009 that I was invited back again. This time it was for a 'four-day stay', a period of time to see if you were suited to life in the hospital.

It was magic, and after some rigorous interviews to see if I was suitable too, I was offered the chance of a position at the hospital.

On 10 March 2009 I was entered as the first lady in-pensioner of the Royal Chelsea Hospital (along with another former woman soldier, Dorothy Hughes), a title I was so proud to accept.

Now I have lived here for over three years and I'm as happy as I have ever been. I feel so very lucky to be staying in such an illustrious place, with people who care, and I am so proud to wear my scarlet coat. I feel part of a family here, a family of ex-servicemen (and, thanks to me, a couple of women!) who have given part of their lives for their country and are still happy to represent an era today.

I was thrilled to spot my old General, Sir Antony Read, in a portrait on the wall when I arrived. Unbeknown to me he was once a governor of this place, so in some ways it feels as if I've come full circle. And of course, I also have my photo of George on the wall, the one I have carried with me all these years of him in his civvies. It takes pride of place above my desk and is placed next to a photo of his gravestone now. From time to time I hear about old comrades through the boys in the home. Once, someone told me they'd served alongside Cedric, who became a Beefeater, bless him, although he's sadly no longer with us. I also still chat to Dawn's husband Harry, after she passed away, and a few others, including Rosemary, my former General's daughter also comes to visit on occasion. How wonderful it is to keep up with some of the lovely people I met along the way.

All in all, joining the army was the most wonderful thing for me. I will spend the rest of my life in the Royal Hospital and I feel very proud to have arrived at such a perfect destination after the journey I've had.